D1245448

INTERCONNECTED

Tropical Biodiversity of St. John, U.S. Virgin Islands

CYNTHIA MOULTON

Original Artwork by Sarah Wyatt

A Naturalist's Week Series

Lulu Publishing Services rev. date: 7/11/2016

For Jess and Ethan

CONTENTS

ACKNOWLEDGMENTS

So many wonderful people helped make this book happen. First of all, I'm grateful to Castleton University for the opportunity to teach a class where I get to bring students to a tropical paradise year after year. I want to thank all the many students from Castleton who took my classes and came along on one trip or another. I learned from each and every one of you. Fellow faculty members Liza Myers, Sherry Crawford, Jeanne Albert, Flo Keyes, and Pat Keller have accompanied me on various trips, and I thank you for helping me manage our crews of students and for offering your insights on all sorts of things.

I'm indebted to Randy Brown for having the vision and determination to take the Virgin Islands Environmental Resource Station (VIERS) from a little-known tropical field station to the research and education center it is now. His support and encouragement were invaluable. I thank Tony and Carla Blackwell, as well as Asya Simons, also from VIERS, who managed the camp during the writing of this book and always made me feel like I was returning home to family. VIERS runs smoothly because of the volunteers I've met during the last decade, including Nancy Prentis, LaVonne Christianson, Liz Pudlak, Lauren Liddy, Patrick Vojnyk, Tucker Stone, Willy and Debbie Moore, Pete and Laura Regan, Barb and Jim Herman, John, and Maryanne.

I'd like to thank the rangers of the National Park Service: Alana, Laurel, Corrine, David, and the others. From St. John, I'd like to thank Ital for his music and knowledge of local plants, Steve Simonsen for his expert advice on photography, and Hamilton Eugene for being the most dependable taxi driver I've ever met. I'm grateful to the Friends of the Virgin Island National Park for supporting kids and making the Virgin

Islands Eco-Camps something that many kids on the island look forward to each summer.

I'm so grateful to Gleb Glinka, a great friend to my husband and me, as well as a superb editor. Finally, I couldn't have done any of this without the loving support of my amazing husband, Jess, and the best son any mother could ever have, Ethan.

INTRODUCTION

Discover a world full of intrigue and drama, history and promise, restfulness and adrenaline. Through these pages I invite you to spend a week in the US Virgin Islands, specifically St. John. We'll investigate diverse and curious animal interactions in shallow reefs, among mangrove roots, on sea grass beds, in dry scrub cactus fields, and along trailside forests.

If you've ever wondered, "What animal is that? What is it doing here? Why would it do that?" then you're a bit like me. Delving a little deeper into the interconnected relationships between the plants and animals of this island has been my endeavor for more than fifteen years. In some instances, I bring minute details into sharper focus; on other occasions, I broaden the lens and present the larger picture. By taking you to some of the different places I visit while here on St. John, my goal is to entertain, educate, and engage you.

Ideally, you really are here, and you can physically visit these locations. If you aren't, why not Google some images of the places and animals mentioned and pretend you're here. Maybe you've already been here, and these pages will bring you back, or perhaps you're deciding to visit. In any case, this book is for you. You don't have to be a naturalist to care about nature, and you don't have to be an expert to appreciate the distinctive lives of animals.

I've organized the book by day, beginning with our arrival. Although each chapter takes you to a location, there are more places to visit. You may actually plan a trip to St. John. You aren't limited to the places mentioned in this book; there are also beautiful beaches on the North Shore and lots of trails you can check out that I haven't mentioned.

Consider booking an organized snorkel tour from one of the many boats that offer trips to some of the outer cays. The National Park Service offers ranger-led programs, like the bird walk at Francis Bay, the water's edge walk in Leinster Bay, and the cultural demonstrations at Annaberg. I encourage you to participate in all of these excellent endeavors.

You don't have to be in fantastic shape to do any of the outings that I've highlighted in these pages, but it helps to be an active-minded person. I like to make sure I have time to read, paint, write in my journal, and relax. It's your trip, though, so experience it as quickly or as slowly, as packed or as sparse as you like. There are wonderful field guides for the sea life, plants, and animals around the island, and this book is obviously not one of them. At the end of the book I've listed some helpful resources that I've used.

One final note: It may not be grammatically correct, but I capitalize the names of plants, trees, fish, and other creatures in this book, such as White-tailed Deer but not deer as a general term. I do this to honor the fact that it's a name, albeit a common name, and not simply a descriptor.

Day One

When we try to pick out anything by itself
we find that it is bound fast by a thousand
invisible cords that cannot be broken,
to everything in the universe.

John Muir
Journal entry for July 27, 1868

Frigate Birds

CHAPTER 1

Cruz Bay

There are only a few ways to get to St. John, and they all involve a boat. Well, I suppose there may be a couple of people that use a helicopter, but to be fair, they're probably returning from a medical transport. So, for all intents and purposes, we'll consider floating as opposed to flying, driving, or walking as the way one would arrive in St. John.

The island is one of the US Virgin Islands. Though the area is a US territory and the people born in the islands are US citizens, they can't vote in a presidential election. The United States purchased St. John from the Danish government in 1917, and at the time, many of the residents were either former slaves or their descendants, with a heritage of proud, progressive, and thoroughly badass ancestors.

The very first slave revolt in the New World occurred on St. John in 1733, and for six glorious and possibly grueling months, the Africans were no longer slaves to white Danish sugar-cane plantation owners. It wasn't until French colonists from Martinique came to the aid of the Danes that the rebellion was quashed. For another 115 years, slavery, however morally abhorrent, remained legal. I recall all this history when I stand at the Annaberg Ruins or the top of Ram Head or on the beach at Cinnamon Bay. St. John is amazingly beautiful, but it hasn't always been paradise— certainly not for everyone.

I usually take the ferry to Cruz Bay from Red Hook, St. Thomas. I could take the Charlotte Amalie ferry, but my flight doesn't arrive in time for the boat ride from the capital, which is closer to the airport but farther from Cruz Bay. Four miles or so and twenty minutes bring me from St. Thomas to St. John. Frigate birds and Brown Boobies flying over the ferry, along with the warm wind, turquoise blue water, and Coconut Palms in the distance—they all sing to me that I'm now in the tropics. At 18°N and 64°W, I find myself in the western Atlantic, the Caribbean Sea, on an island that looks like a long-dormant yet verdant volcano sculpted by waves, earthquakes, uplifts, and winds. This is not an island that will disappear with the rise of a few inches in sea level, although the beaches would.

The ferry pulls in to the dock, and the bay is full of smaller sailboats, skiffs, and motorboats. These boats are actually used and loved, not just adored from the shore. I look for some familiar vessels, and I see the *Sadie Sea* and *Bad Kitty* bobbing on the waves in the harbor. As seaside beach towns go, Cruz Bay is eclectic and about as charming as they get. It's always bustling with a mixture of tourists, locals, and taxi drivers.

For getting around the island, Hamilton is the one man I call when I bring my college classes to St. John. He's a local but not a native. He was born in St. Lucia and has been everywhere in the world. My students see a friendly, carefree guy—a lot of "no problem" and "don't worry"—but I see a savvy and remarkably reliable businessman. When he says he'll pick us up at 1 p.m., he means he'll be there at 12:30 p.m. He makes you feel like you're on island time when you're in his taxi, but he never forgets that he's on the clock. That's the magic of successful tourism. You feel like everyone is your friend, but the reality is, in one or two weeks you'll be gone, and a new friend will replace you—hopefully.

I'm not going to the Westin or Gallows Point or any one of the hordes of villas you can rent but to the Virgin Islands Environmental Resource Station, also known as VIERS. Traveling east on Center Line Road, the trip to VIERS is about seventeen miles and takes almost an hour. The road twists with upward sloping bends, then curves with steep declines, and the left-side driving makes it all a little more adventurous, especially for the uninitiated.

Even in the dry season (February and March), beautiful, bright hues fill the air from the vibrant-green Mother-in-Law Tongues to the pink Coral Vine to the yellow blossoms of the Ginger Thomas, the official flower of the US Virgin Islands (USVI). As you drive around the island, notice the bougainvillea, which is a thorny bush with what appear to be fuchsia flowers. As it happens, the flowers are really the tiny white structures poking out from the leaves. The pink "petals" are actually spring leaves.

From your vantage point, don't be surprised to see donkeys, sheep, or goats wandering on the side of the road. In the branches of a tree, you might notice a big brown blob as if the trunk is growing an enormous tumor. Don't be alarmed. It's only a termite nest, and they don't hurt the tree at all. Although there may be as many as twenty-one different species of termites on the island, the ones that make these huge nests are Nasute Termites, or *Nasutitermes acajutlae*.

The workers care for the young, build the nest, and create little tunnels. Working within these covered trails, the termites are protected from both the sun and their predators, which are mostly ants, other bugs, birds, anoles, and other lizards. The soldiers guard the workers, but their weapon is a trumpet-shaped face that blows a sticky substance onto their predators. No biting at all. The workers have mandibles, but they use them to chomp up and recycle fallen wood into the organic matter useful to plants and other tiny organisms. The Nasute Termites have a job to do in tropical forests; without them, detritus and dead vegetation would simply lie on the ground, useless to the regenerative process of nutrient cycling.

About a half mile after passing by the Salt Pond Bay beach parking area, the road inclines up an imposing hairpin turn. This climb is not for the faint of heart. In fact, a sign like the one in *The Wizard of Oz*—"I'd turn back if I were you"—used to be at the bottom of this hill. Or was that just my imagination?

Finally, I arrive at VIERS, a quaint, isolated field station consisting of sixteen yellow cabins, including a dining hall and a classroom, the Tektite Museum, a tent-like pavilion, a gazebo, a dock, a lab, and an office. At this writing, Tony and Carla manage the place, with Asya assisting and learning the ropes so as to take over. Technically, Tony is the manager, but Carla is the unsung hero that keeps Tony sane and the Internet working. I hope VIERS will always be this rural camp. While visitors to this field station are managed by a nonprofit organization called Clean Islands International, the whole operation dances between the University of the

Virgin Islands that owns the buildings and the US National Park Service that owns the land on which the buildings sit.

School groups come and stay to learn about marine biology and island ecology. Researchers come and study subjects as diverse as coral reefs, termites, and bats. And the occasional tourist lodges in the screened-in cabins to experience a primitive comfort that's walking distance to the beach.

I'm here, and I take in the sound of frogs and tree crickets. Hermit crabs are shuffling around in the dry, crinkling leaves outside my window. I'm sharing my cabin with an anole, at least one cockroach, and a line of ants marching across the room to a hole through which the sink pipe extends in the bathroom floor. I watch them and decide to stay out of their way to let them reach their destination. After all, how many ants can there be?

CHAPTER 2

VIERS

Mangos are ripening on the tree next to Cabin Nine, so the White-tail Deer are hanging around camp. Guests are in and out of the cabins. Though the staff encourages people to close the doors gently, inevitably people forget, and *slam*, a door bounces on its hinges. It spooks the deer, and their sudden movements in the dry leaves are like a false start for a hundred-meter race.

There are researchers here collecting deer pellets and setting out barbed wire to capture deer hair samples. Actually, a lot can be gleaned from deer poop. There are some logical conclusions: more piles probably mean more deer; wetter poop is more recently plopped; a bigger pile indicates a larger animal. But aside from what a hunter or tracker might deduce, scientists can examine the pellets and assess the pathogen load of an individual deer and dietary information like the quantities of specific plants a doe or a buck has ingested.

So these four-legged, dainty beasts are in and around the camp and down by Lameshur Bay. Seeing deer at a beach is just cool. Maybe it's because I come from Vermont, and I think of deer as woodland and field creatures. On islands their options are more limited, and they're considerably smaller. They often travel in little groups of two or three, and when you see them, they give you a look like "Oh, don't mind me. I'm here just foraging around for a tasty nibble." They step gingerly through the brush and look back at you to make sure you're not following.

These are the descendants of White-tailed Deer brought to the islands in the seventeen hundreds—on purpose—so they might breed and the people might have meat to hunt. Along with the pigs, sheep, goats, donkeys, and cows that traveled along with humans, these animals were welcomed and useful at the time. Cats and dogs came later, but rats and mice were uninvited travel companions.

Unfortunately, those tagalong rodents caused damage and disease, and they ate sugar cane profits so unrestrainedly that caused someone to say, "I know, let's get some Asian Mongooses. Someone brought them to Jamaica for the rats that eat cane, so we should too!" Although these mongooses successfully reduced the impact of rodents on sugar plantations in the 1700s and 1800s, they have now become a problem.

Asian Mongooses are not rodents, but are included in a group of mammals referred to as the *Carnivora* (along with wolves, tigers, and mink). And like some other carnivores, they have voracious appetites; they'll eat almost any living egg or animal *and*, as it turns out, sugar cane, other crops, and your idle sandwich. Also the likes of sea turtle eggs and ground-nesting birds, anoles, iguanas, crabs, snakes, piglets, poultry, fruits of all kind, and—well, you see where this is going. All have suffered the unintended consequences of yet another brilliant demonstration of human ingenuity.

So a question looms: What do we do about it? Do we let the mongoose run amok to devour baby animals and decimate populations of innocent species? Or do we value the individual rights of mongooses and say what's done is done, suffering the consequences. But people don't suffer. In fact, the first time I saw a mongoose, I was excited. They're cute, and they run fast, and somewhere I heard that they can kill a cobra.

Mongooses are actually amusing, and there is a shopping plaza in Cruz Bay named in their honor. At issue is the fact that humans did this, but it's the natural ecosystem that must pay the price. The descendants of the island's first mongoose inhabitants had a nice run, but it's time for it to end. And I feel a little sorry about it, because every creature involved—from the sea turtles and the Least terns that no longer nest on St. John, to the endangered Virgin Island Tree Boa, to the mongooses that caused all of this devastation—are innocent victims.

Every mammal you see on St. John, with the exception of bats and humans, is an introduced species. You might hear the term *exotic*, which refers to a species that arrives at a new destination by accident, or on purpose, because of people. It may not have any natural predators in this new place, so it can become an invasive species, though not all exotic species become a problem.

Bats are "native" species because they came to the island on their own. It helps that they fly. Bats belong to a group of mammals called the *Chiroptera*, derived from the Latin, *chiro*, meaning hand, and the Greek *pteron*, meaning wing. This alludes to the long finger bones within their membranous wings.

A point of clarification: bats *can* see. In fact, they can see about as well as humans. But because they fly around at night, they need extra help in avoiding objects; so they have evolved to use echolocation as well. Try riding your bike at night without lights (please, don't really do this), and you'll get a sense of what it might be like to be limited to using only your vision to find small food items. You can imagine that acute hearing would come in super handy.

According to Renata Platenburg, a professor at the University of the Virgin Islands, as many as six species of bats might be found in and around St. John. The most common chiropteran is the Jamaican Fruit-eating Bat, which is similar to the Antillean Fruit-eating Bat, and the locally endangered Red Fig-eating Bat. Since these bats eat fruit, they disperse seeds and help pollinate trees.

Next time you're at the sugar ruins of Reef Bay, go inside the dilapidated building and look up. If you don't say awwwwh at the sight of little bats snuggling up with each other in the rafters, don't read the rest of this chapter. For those of you still with me, these bats are Antillean Fruit-eating bats, and like most species of bats in the world, their numbers seem to be dwindling.

The bat most likely to take up residence in an attic of an island home or a specially made bat house is Pallas's Mastiff Bat, also known as the Mosquito Bat or Roof Bat. Catching insects in-flight is elegant work, and this species eats lots of them. They have a cute pug nose, and they're the smallest bat on the island. Their body is only two inches or so long, and they have a wingspan of about twelve inches.

Occasionally, a Mexican Free-tail Bat flitters around the island—so called because their tail makes up about half of their length and extends well beyond their uropatagium (which is the scientific word for wing membrane). They like big, crowded, cave-like roosts, like the ones in Puerto Rico, so they would just be visiting St. John (no big caves here). You might be familiar with the image of this bat as the icon of Bacardi rum.

Last but not least, my favorite bat of all is the Greater Bulldog Bat, which is sometimes referred to as the Fishing Bat. As flying mammals go, this bat is huge, with a wingspan of up to two feet. A Bulldog Bat can grab a fish right out of the ocean with its feet. Flying above the water, it uses echolocation to identify ripples in the water created by schools of small fish. Making sweeps of fifty centimeters to three meters, the bat uses its talons to snatch fish from the water, as many as twenty-five in one night. If you ever have the chance, stand on Europa Point at sunset. Be quiet and still, and prepare to be amazed.

Day Two

Because there's nothing more beautiful
than the way the ocean refuses
to stop kissing the shoreline,
no matter how many times it's sent away.
Sarah Kay

Asian Mongoose

CHAPTER 3

Little Lameshur Bay

Strap a mask to your head, place a snorkel in your mouth, put your face in the water, and glide. Try it. Now try to do it without smiling, because the upturn of your lips will make the water fill your mask.

The sea around St. John is saltier than you might expect, even for the ocean, but that just means it's easier to float on. Seriously, stop smiling. At Little Lameshur Bay, you can snorkel right from the beach, close to shore. You don't even have to know how to swim. Just breathe.

Snorkeling allows us to see a whole new circumstance for life and changes the way we see ourselves in the world. No longer are we the masters of the universe; we're just slightly hairy trunks with spindly arms and legs that really have no business feeling superior. Sea turtles, with their cumbersome shells and flipper feet, are like ballerinas in the ocean. Butterfly Fish glide effortlessly in and around coral and sea fans with barely perceptible movements of their fins and tail. Even the Long-spined Sea Urchins, seemingly sessile, shift position using their hundreds of tube feet while harboring baby puffer fish and Mysid Shrimp between their spikes.

The shallow waters just off the beach at Lameshur Bay hold a majestic, beautiful community of creatures that exist unaware of test scores, car payments, and online shopping. First you'll notice the fish. One minute you're fixing the straps on your mask, and the next minute you're looking underwater at a little finned swimmer that has been there the whole time.

That fish noticed you immediately. He probably checked near your feet to see if you stirred up any tiny plankton that had previously lodged in the sand. As your heavy legs make strange turbulence in the water, you might liberate even more tiny prey, and you could have four or five fish near you in a matter of minutes. Be sure to watch them.

Most people want to start swimming immediately to see the bigger fish that hang out on the edges of the bay, toward the rocky shores off Yawzi Point. I heartily recommend doing that—in a minute. For now, notice the tiny damselfish with their jewel-like blue and yellow bodies, guarding their place near a tiny coral head or rocky spot. Be amused by the Slippery Dicks (yes, that's really what they're called), with their red and green stripes, nipping at the invisible life among the odd plants that grow in the shallows, mermaids' fans, and Neptune's shaving brushes.

Appreciate the Sergeant Majors. From juveniles about as big as a quarter nearer to the shore to adults about the size of a dinner plate out further, all have five black bars on their yellow-splashed white bodies. Unlike other fish, Sergeant Majors look mainly the same from individual to individual and from young to mature, so they're easy to identify and often the first fish my students recognize.

Before we come to St. John, I ask my class to paint about twenty species of common fish that we'll see while we're here. When you've painted a picture from a photo, seeing your subject in real life is thrilling; it's like bumping into an old friend in a distant airport or seeing a movie star walk into the restaurant you happen to be eating at. Drawing the fish ahead of time allows you to spot the familiar and gradually transforms the image you had in your mind to the one that's right in front of you. A connection is formed and a bond solidified.

Something about seeing and recognizing the inhabitants of the sea leads to feeling protective toward it. Now it's not just a pretty beach with turquoise blue water; it's a home to a myriad of different species that struggle and triumph. These are fish that have to find enough sustenance and secure places to lay their eggs, to show off for the opposite sex, and to avoid becoming food. They have to contend with the natural population fluctuations: the lows of their prey as well as the highs of their predators. They deal with the effects of tropical storms and hurricanes as well as the daily variations of temperature within their habitat.

In addition, as people become more pervasive, sea life has had to cope with influxes of toxins (from rat poison to bug sprays), sediments from road and building development, freshwater runoff from increased amounts of impervious surfaces (which dilutes the salinity in their habitat), and the added noise of engines, voices, music, etc. I wonder what impression we humans make on these creatures that share the earth and sea with us. I can't help thinking that from their perspective, *we* must be incredibly annoying pests. And I imagine when we are at our best and our impacts are mild, the creatures of the sea perform a collective eye roll with a bit of head shaking. But when people pull their most rueful acts, I imagine their response must be an all-out community panic attack.

Anthropomorphizing aside, sea life is at the mercy of human compassion, morality, greed, impatience, and indifference. The oceans are at a disadvantage because we don't really see what's going on under the water. Think about the human condition. Scenario one: You come upon a clear-cut, bulldozed forest where there are bodies of chipmunks and raccoons, song birds, monarch butterflies, and trees lying dead everywhere. You discover that the culprits of this destruction were rabbit hunters. To ensure that all the rabbits in the area were found, they had to bring about the demise of the entire habitat.

Who would put up with this? Almost anyone who would come upon this hypothetical scene would cry out, "This is an outrage, and we can't allow this! Look at what has become of this section of the forest!" Fortunately, scenario one is not something that would really happen.

Now consider scenario two: You come upon an area under water that has just been trawled. Two boats dragged a weighted rope on the bottom of the ocean, and in their wake, baby sharks, flounder, parrotfish, Sergeant Majors, sponges, coral, conch, and a sea turtle float helplessly dead or dying, and their ocean habitat is destroyed. You discover that the culprits of this destruction were harvesting shrimp. Do the same rules of fairness and morality apply? If you wouldn't allow this on land, surely it would be as much of an outrage to have this happen under water.

Unfortunately, this is not the case. Apparently, this method of fishing is *controversial*; government agencies are debating how to regulate it. What? How is this okay? It's okay because we don't have to look at it. We don't drive by it on our way to work or school. Our children don't have to see the consequences and question why we don't protect the baby sharks.

If we had to hunt for our meat this way, it wouldn't take long before there would be no more habitat for our meat to live in. So we've turned to raising it rather than hunting it. Our oceans are far more vast than our forests. We could harvest fish or shrimp this way for longer than we could in terrestrial areas before there would be no more suitable habitat for our fish to live in.

It's interesting that we use the word *harvest* to refer to fishing at all. Do commercial fishermen tend and nurture the fish stocks for part of the year to reap a harvest when the time is right? Are they like farmers I know, caretakers of the soils and pastures, nurturing the species that reside on their land? If there are some, I'd like to meet you.

Breathe, because for now, you're snorkeling in Little Lameshur Bay, and there is no shrimp trawling here or anywhere in the Virgin Islands National Park. Learn the names of the fish you see. Watch them for a while, and try to figure out what they're doing. Think about where you see a particular species. Does it hang out under a rock like a Nassau Grouper, or is it visiting little outcroppings and picking a few morsels off each one, like a French Angelfish? Does it float motionless as if suspended by a string like a Barracuda, or is it sitting on top of the sand like a Sand Diver? Is it in a school, or is it alone? Mind the sea urchins and the Fire Coral; they're part of this community too. Be a respectful guest. And when you get out of the water and take off your mask, smile as much as you'd like.

Four-Eye Butterfly Fish

CHAPTER 4

Yawzi Point

A rocky peninsula separates Greater and Little Lameshur Bays, known as Yawzi Point. A short trail leads to a gratifying view as you wander along the way through a channel of Organ Pipe cactuses and carcasses of Century plants. I remember only a decade ago when the Century plants on Yawzi made a magical border along the path, but because of a tiny beetle, the Mexican Snout Beetle, the once mighty Century plant now struggles to maintain a presence on the island.

The beetle, also known as the Agave Snout Weevil, was introduced to St. John in the early 2000s by way of infected cultivated agaves brought into Tortola. Like all weevils, they can fly, so this pest hopscotched its way through the British and US Virgin Islands, Puerto Rico, and beyond. The half-inch long female uses her "snout" to puncture a hole in the base of the century plant, where she lays her eggs. Microbes associated with the weevils begin decomposing the plant tissue; when the eggs hatch, the tiny, white grub-like babies feast on the decaying plant innards. This is the same pest that attacks the Century plant's cousin, the Blue Agave, which is cultivated to make tequila. Traditionally, this grub is the "worm" inside the tequila bottle.

The weevil and the Century plant provide an example of an ecological relationship between a predator with an extremely high rate of reproduction taking advantage of its newly found and abundant prey. Unfortunately, this food source has an extremely slow reproductive rate. Although one blooming Century plant can release hundreds, perhaps thousands, of seeds, it flowers only once in its lifetime, taking ten to twenty years to produce that single stalk of yellow glory. It can also send out shoots from its roots, but because these are so close to the infected parent, often the nearby plants are afflicted quickly.

Perhaps the Century plant can rebound. If a few pockets of uninfected plants are allowed to thrive free of pests, the weevil population could reach a sort of equilibrium, or even die out. I'm hopeful for this, because this fast-reproducing population also has one disadvantage: each weevil has a short life span. This may turn out to be a race between the turtle and the hare; we just have to make sure there is still habitat available for the Century plant at the end of this race. For now, the towering Organ Pipe cactuses still line the path, along with other interesting vegetation like Frangipani trees and Turks Cap cactuses. Just watch out for cactus spines.

Farther along the trail, two crumbling foundations sit prominently about halfway down the peninsula. I've been told numerous times that in the old days, slaves with Yawzi disease came to live and be quarantined in the houses that used to be here. Yaws, a disease similar to leprosy, afflicts the skin with lesions, scaling, and disfigurement. Neither disease is highly contagious, requiring close physical contact to spread person to person— that is, skin-to-skin touching. Also, both diseases are treatable *now*, when they are diagnosed in the early stages.

Yaws was certainly a disease that heavily impacted the Caribbean, along with many other countries between the Tropics of Cancer and Capricorn. Its impact was, and still is, worse on people who live in close proximity with other people and lack a high standard of hygiene. Add to these conditions extensive areas of vegetation, and it starts to sound like conditions on St. John during the 1700s and 1800s. (Think sugar cane, cotton, and slavery.)

The chain of title for this peninsula began in 1720 when the land was identified as a modest cotton plantation. In 1732 Gewert Marche purchased what is now known as Yawzi Point, where he lived with his wife, Suzanna, and twelve slaves. A dwelling house, a pack house (to dry cotton), and slave quarters existed until 1748, when the two plantation buildings burned to the ground and the owners "died." It seems that neither building was ever rebuilt while the land continued to change hands.

The old deed records culminate with Herman Creque, who purchased the land in 1930 to raise livestock and was noted to have 250 head of cattle.

Still, the name Yawzi Point hadn't yet been used. The inventory of Estate Lameshur in the late 1700s referenced a sick house, though it's not clear where exactly on the 235 acres it was located.

We can always perpetuate a good rumor: a quarantine camp on the peninsula may be a plausible scenario, even if there is scant evidence for it. There were lots of diseases that might warrant keeping a sick house, infirmary, or other such isolating quarters near the main house. Someone, perhaps a child, who lived in one of those houses could have played in the vegetation after a long rain and scraped his leg on one of the curved spines of the Century plants. It wouldn't have taken long for his skin to look bumpy at the site of the wound. Within the boy's skin, the bacteria would flourish, and inadvertently he would infect his entire family. It may have been an event noteworthy enough so that the peninsula became known as Yawzi Point, albeit that's total conjecture. (The St. John's Historical Society has detailed records of the area, and a 2007 article by David W. Knight Sr. may be accessed through its website.)

Back to the present. Let's proceed and turn left at the side trail leading down to a little cove facing Greater Lameshur Bay. The waves rush in between two high, close-set rocks standing about a meter or so from shore. Between the rock alley and the water's edge is a fairly shallow but swirly pool. Perhaps you'd like to climb on the oversized boulders and admire the boats in the bay or pelicans fishing, but I'd suggest you also pull out your snorkeling gear. Although it's really shallow here, you're still going to want to lie down flat in the water. Straighten your legs and guide yourself through the rock opening. Time it right, and you'll be whisked between the rocks into a second deeper pool, but be mindful of your fins and avoid kicking your feet; otherwise you'll probably jam them into something.

I saw my first cleaning station in this spot. A Princess Parrotfish, turquoise blue with a splash of yellow, floated in an upward slant with his mouth open while three black- and gold-striped gobies plucked tiny bites along his body. Next a Blue-striped Grunt sidled in, and a juvenile French Angelfish joined the gobies in picking at the grunt's scales. I moved, and all the fish scattered. The show was over, and I never saw a cleaning station in that exact spot again. These stations aren't fixed; some are just a moment in time.

I've snorkeled this site many times, and sometimes it's churning with sediment while other times it's the highlight of my trip. The walls of rock create a maze of Dijon mustard–colored Fire Coral, Mat Zoanthids, and patches of Christmas Tree Worms and Feather Dusters. There are whip-like Gorgonians and Purple Sea Fans, a few large Elkhorn Coral, and a beaten-up Brain Coral. It's real life, not a pristine tank, so the organisms in this area show their wear and tear from disease, storms, predation, and age.

The usual suspects are here. A gang of Blue Tangs, some brilliant, sapphire blue, others pale and powdery, maraud the territories of damselfish for algae and other vegetation. From knobs of coral protruding from the sand, a pair of Four-eyed Butterfly Fish deliberately plucks tasty morsels from within the polyps. A school of French Grunts hangs out near a sea fan as though they're just waiting for a game to begin. And the parrotfish, in their various stages of adulthood, are numerous, though only the terminal males have the fantastic colorations that make them easy to identify by species. I have encountered brilliant Triggerfish, Porcupine Fish with their huge, soft eyes, Trumpet Fish hanging upside down, and the oddly shaped Trunk Fish. But the day is always a success if a Hawksbill Sea Turtle enters the scene. Seeing a sea turtle coasting effortlessly under the water makes time stop for a moment. Today I'm especially lucky, because as a massive Spotted Eagle Ray sails past, my heart fills with awe, and just a little fear.

The guidebooks and coral reef videos didn't prepare me for the grace and beauty of sea creatures going about their daily business. As a human, moving around in the water is like being the biggest klutz in a room full of dancers. At best I just hope they ignore me, because I want to keep watching them, observing their routines without freaking the fish out.

Yet now, having been in the water for over two hours, I'm starting to get cold, even though I'm wearing a full-length rash guard. The suit helps with warmth, though I mainly wear it because there isn't enough sunscreen in the world to protect my freckled pale skin from sunburn. Also, it's easy to get dehydrated while snorkeling, because you're immersed in water, yet with the sun and all that mouth breathing, you can lose a lot of internal fluid.

I figure it's time to go back. I swim to shore, allowing the waves to push me through the rock gateway to the cove. I put my flip-flops back on, gather my stuff, and continue to the end of Yawzi Point. I've saved some of my water for this spot, and I take a long drink, savoring the view and quenching my thirst. I decide to come back again at sunset.

Day Three

The sea, once it casts its spell,
holds one in its net of wonder forever.
Jacques Cousteau

Nassau Grouper

CHAPTER 5

Greater Lameshur Bay

The beach is rocky with stones ranging in proportions from pea-size to softballs, making barefoot walking almost impossible. Not to mention the bits of jagged, broken, bleached coral intermingling with the rocks, along with pieces of dried sponges and skeletons of sea fans. There are no manicured coconut palms; here the beach is littered with trees like the thorny acacia, the sea grape, and buttonbush. The shade cast from these trees creates the favored places for beach fleas and no-see-ums. At the shore, sea urchins speckle the shallows, and Sargasso Weed is strewn along the water's edge. This disheveled beach is a snorkeler's paradise!

It's interesting that two beaches can be as close as Greater and Little Lameshur Bays yet still have completely different attributes. While Little Lameshur has soft white sand and lapping waves, Greater Lameshur has rocks, broken shells, and fragments of coral that make sitting on a towel literally a pain in the—well, you know.

This difference is due in part to the amount of wave energy that hits these two beaches. The angles they face toward the open ocean and the land formations that protect them regulate the wave action that pummels the shore. On Greater Lameshur, the energy is higher, resulting in larger items being deposited on the shore, like big stones and huge breaks of coral that get whittled to round cobble from constantly grinding against one another.

The lower-energy waves on Little Lameshur allow small particles in the water to settle on the beach as the waves wash over the gently sloping coastline. These fine sediments include tiny bits of rock weathered over time, calcium carbonate from nicked chunks of coral and shells ground small through the years, silica spicules of sponges long dead as well as the clouds of ground-up coral you might notice coming out of the parrotfish after they've digested the algae and flesh of coral polyps. Yes, the beautiful white sands of some of the most photographed beaches in the world are bits of rock, glass, coral, and parrotfish poop.

Wave energy drives the particles in the water to move about and nourish the organisms that live among the crevasses and valleys in the sea floor. These dips and ridges create microenvironments where a coral can get a foothold or an oyster can find protection. Over time, the hard surfaces of oysters and coral become attachment points for the marine worms and sponges, which later become food and habitat for fish, shrimp, and crabs. Although most people focus on fish when they snorkel, the sea is a complex and diverse mixture of fantastic animal life. One fish's food is another fish's home, while the eggs and juvenile stages of fish become food for the corals and marine worms.

In the undersea community of Greater Lameshur Bay are thousands of individual, under-appreciated marine worms. Bristle Worms lumber across coral heads, plucking off tiny copepods with their pincer-like faces. Their segmented bodies are lined with parapodia. Parapodia (the singular form is *parapodium*) look like little paddle-like flaps on the flanks of each segment. Spines, called setae, that inject poison poke out from under the parapodia, so avoid touching these worms, or you'll get a painful sting that can last a week.

Tube-dwelling polychaetes are also abundant in Greater Lameshur. My favorite are the Christmas Tree Worms, aptly named because their feeding structures appear as two colorful spiral crowns resembling, yes, you guessed it: Christmas trees. These structures are called radioles and are used in feeding and breathing. If touched, they can disappear in an instant inside their hollow parchment tunnel.

There are also Feather Dusters, which also reside in tubes and disguise their heads with a crown of feeding appendages. Their radioles are double-sided sticky combs that nab tiny organisms floating in the water. Radioles work like this: Imagine your forearm covered in milk as you shove your hand down a box of Cheerios. When you remove your arm, it's covered in individual Cheerios stuck to the milk that clings to your skin. Moving your arm to your mouth allows your lips to quickly and easily pluck off each morsel of toasty oat goodness one by one. It's messier than a spoon, but it works.

There are Spaghetti Worms too, which look like long strands of clear pasta, except that that's only the part you see. The actual worm lives in a burrow and has a plump, segmented body. The parts that look like spaghetti are actually gummy tentacles that accrue bits of food as they float by. The Spaghetti Worm expends almost no energy because its food floats by and gets tangled in those long strands. Each strand is shaped like a rain gutter lined with tiny cilia. The practically invisible cilia transport food particles down the length of the tentacle to the mouth, conveyer-belt style.

Marine worms are beautiful and cool, and they inspired filmmaker James Cameron to use their likeness in his movie *Avatar*. Although much of the life history of these worms has yet to be discovered, we do know that they comprise a good portion of the diet of fish species. A study done by Jack Randall and published in 1967 found that the diets of sixty-two species of fish found in Lameshur Bay included, to a significant extent, marine polychaetes. (Note that when I use the word *polychaete*, it's synonymous with the word *worm*.) Randall's paper can be found at http://www.aoml.noaa.gov/general/lib/CREWS/Cleo/PuertoRico/ prpdfs/randall-habits.pdf, if you're interested in a more thorough explanation of the dining preferences of fish in the Caribbean.

My friend Nancy Prentiss, a professor from the University of Maine at Farmington, studies marine worms. The number and variety of species of polycheates in Greater Lameshur Bay is staggering. She has discovered new species right here and in other bays of St. John. In her work, she snorkels, turns over a lot of rocks, and collects sand from various places, including from within the bowls of sponges. Later, on dry land, she patiently sifts through samples under a microscope. She has a National Park Service research permit to allow her to collect and keep her specimens; her permit has many conditions that ensure the park's resources are protected. Interestingly, her permit also requires her to capture and kill any Lionfish she encounters while conducting her marine worm research.

Unfortunately, Lionfish have also found Greater Lameshur Bay. For their beauty and ferocity, aquarists have prized these natives to the Pacific and Indian Oceans. Their spiny dorsal fins carry a toxin that, though not usually fatal to humans, is extremely painful and can make you nauseous and disrupt your breathing. Although Lionfish are voracious predators, they have few enemies in St. John, because they have lived here only since around 2010.

The Gulf and Caribbean Fisheries Institute (GCFI) has an interesting website that shows a timeline for when Lionfish were first discovered in the Atlantic (near Fort Lauderdale, Florida) and when and where they have premiered in other parts of the Atlantic. (Go to http://lionfish.gcfi.org/.) The adverse impact of Lionfish on local fisheries has been documented for many locations, and the National Park Service takes their invasion of the Virgin Islands National Park very seriously. Lionfish precisely fit the definition of an invasive species because they have very few natural predators in the Atlantic, they have a high reproductive rate, and they compete with and displace native fish for food resources.

The Caribbean Oceanic Restoration and Education Foundation (CORE) provides support for tracking and extracting Lionfish from Caribbean waters. CORE has worked with fishermen, the first line of defense against Lionfish, and with community members and dive boat operators to remove thousands of Lionfish from Caribbean waters. You too can be part of the solution by reporting any sightings of Lionfish to www.corevi.org/submit.html.

Although Lionfish are edible and tasty if prepared properly, it might not be a good idea to eat Lionfish caught within territorial waters of the Virgin Islands due to Ciguatera Fish Poisoning (CFP). Fish that prey on other reef fish are most likely to accumulate the microalgae *Gambierdiscus toxicus* and other toxin-producing dinoflagellates. Species of these microalgae adhere to coral, so as herbivorous fish eat the algae and coral, and bigger fish eat these herbivores, the toxin moves up the food chain in a process known as biomagnification.

The organisms that produce Ciguatera toxin are associated with coral reefs worldwide, usually in localized areas. Ecological conditions like warm water temperatures and storm surges can cause the dinoflagellates to bloom and spread to other areas. For CFP, or Ciguatera, there is a long list of symptoms beginning with gastrointestinal distress and lingering neurological effects. Symptoms can last for weeks, and the neurological issues can sometimes last for years, perhaps through repeated exposures or other triggers. There is no known cure.

There are some folk methods used to determine if a fish is contaminated with Ciguatera, but these haven't been shown by scientific tests to be a reliable way to determine toxicity. The coral reefs around the Virgin Islands and nearby islands are prime habitat for these toxin-bearing microbes, so avoiding large reef carnivores—like barracuda, grouper, snapper, or mackerel—is probably a wise choice.

CHAPTER 6

Tektite

Tektites are small glass spheres that form as a meteor crashes into the Earth's surface. They're found in only a few places in the world, usually within the strewn field of a meteor impact, which can be hundreds—even thousands—of kilometers long. In addition, microtektites have been discovered in core sediments from the ocean bottom.

Scientists initially thought tektites were a sort of extraterrestrial space glass because their composition is so unlike anything else found on earth. But now geologists acknowledge them to be completely comprised of ejected terrestrial debris. In other words, when a meteor hits the earth, the high heat and pressure of the cratering event actually liquefies rock and soil on contact. This molten debris cools to form the glass pellets we refer to as tektites.

Tektite was also the name of one of the earliest manned undersea habitats, which was situated in the waters off Cabritte Horn Point between Greater Lameshur Bay and Grootpan Bay in St. John. Designed and built by General Electric, the habitat was fairly small with two cylinder-shaped chambers, each four meters in diameter and six meters tall, connected by a passageway tunnel between them. Each cylinder consisted of two floors. One cylinder contained the crew's living quarters with bunks and a kitchen on the lower level, with the bridge in the upper floor. The other cylinder comprised the equipment room and dry lab on the upper floor with the wet room on the lower level. The aquanauts entered through a hatch in the wet room.)For a more in-depth look at the construction and design of the Tektite habitat, check out the July 17, 2014, article by Dr. Frank A. Blazich, Jr. in the official online magazine of the SeaBees (http://seabeemagazine.navylive.dodlive.mil/2014/07/17/project-tektite-i-and-the-birth-of-the-underwater-construction-teams/). The link between outer space and the ocean is poignant because the missions involving the habitat capsule known as Tektite played a crucial role in the future of both space travel and undersea research.

Tektite I was a joint mission between the US Navy, the National Aeronautics and Space Administration (NASA), and the Department of the Interior (DOI). The navy was interested in ocean technology, NASA was concerned about the psychological effects of living in a confined area with no reasonable hope of escape (think space station), and the DOI got involved because they wanted to be able to conduct research in the ocean that extended the depth and time marine scientists could work on the sea floor. By the end of the sixty-day mission, Aquanauts Ed Clifton, Conrad Mahnken, Richard Waller, and John VanDerwalker had spent a total of 432 man-hours underwater (the longest saturation dive up to that point). NASA was able to conduct a meaningful study of human behavior that somewhat mimicked the role of astronauts working in space.

Tektite II became the first real underwater scientific laboratory. In 1970 eleven teams of aquanauts, each consisting of four marine scientists and one habitat engineer, ran missions while they lived and worked on the sea floor about fifteen meters below the surface. Each mission was scheduled for between two and four weeks.

There were no physiological or significant medical problems during the missions, and their work opened up possibilities of marine research that hadn't even been thought of before. Incidentally, Tektite II also included an all-female team. According to Randy Brown, founder and curator of the Tektite Underwater Habitat Museum on St. John, the only difference between the men and the women was that the women spent more hours in the water, conducted more research, and discovered more new species than the men's teams.

All of the aquanauts were extremely competent and were selected for the mission based on diving experience, the scientific potential of their work, and their physical condition. It just so happened that the women wore colorful swimsuits and were very photogenic. In fact, the performance of this team of women—Sylvia Earle, Renate True, Ann Hartline, Alina Szmant, and Margaret Ann Lucas—burst open the doors for women in underwater and space missions in the future.

Earle subsequently went on to become one of the most influential women in marine science as she continues her focus on ocean education and conservation to this day. She is the founder of Mission Blue (mission-blue.org/) and hopes to ignite public support to create a global network of marine-protected areas to safeguard the ocean's inhabitants. Her goal is to protect 20 percent of the ocean by 2020.

The habitat used in both Tektite I and II, which was technically owned by General Electric, was later purchased by a group of interested parties for one dollar with the stipulation that it be removed from its storage facility in Philadelphia. For about ten years, schoolchildren in San Francisco were able to tour the habitat. By 1980 it had been refurbished and certified for underwater use. Sadly, funds to submerge and operate the habitat were never allocated. Eventually, some welding school students dismantled the habitat and recycled the metal parts.

In 1966 the place we now think of as VIERS was a base camp built by Navy Seabees to house the men involved in this project, known collectively as Tektite. What began as a series of collected photographs displayed under a tent at the fortieth anniversary of VIERS in 2006 is now a museum in a permanent building with hundreds of photographs, articles, and artifacts of the missions that took place between 1968 and 1970. Organizing, salvaging, and bringing to fruition this bit of St. John history has been a labor of love for the curator and creator of the Tektite Underwater Habitat Museum, Randy Brown.

After you visit the museum, consider taking a kayak out to the actual site of the Tektite habitat. From Greater Lameshur Bay, paddle east to Cabritte Horn Point to a place that Google maps actually refers to as Tektite Bay. If you find yourself in Grootpan Bay, you've gone too far.

The snorkeling here is nice and not very different from a lot of other places on the south shore, except for its historic significance. Now almost anyone can get certified to strap on a tank and breathe underwater to look at fish or shipwrecks. Scuba divers might want to pay their respects by touching the place that marks the spot of Tektite. Thank you, Randy Brown, for bringing this wonderful museum to St. John.

CHAPTER 7

Europa Bay

The spur trail from VIERS merges with the road at just the right spot to see land crabs. On the ocean side of the road, you'll see softball-sized holes. If you're patient and quiet, you'll eventually see one of these skittish arthropods emerge. Activity here intensifies at dusk and at night while they look for fruit and vegetation to eat.

This species is the Great land crab (*Cardisoma guanhumi*), which are large: nearly ten centimeters long—and that's just their main carapace, not including the claws. They possess seven pairs of appendages. These include antennae used for sensory purposes and a pair of maxillapeds that move food to the mouth. Most notable are a pair of chelipeds—what you might think of as arms—each with a claw known as a chela.

One chela is a lot bigger than the other, particularly in males. The muscles of their body actually build up asymmetrically as well. The males use their chela to defend themselves, to show off or to fight with other males, and to perform dramatic claw movements to romance females. The claw is important, and if they lose it, it will eventually grow back. It turns out that carrying around two massive claws takes a lot of energy, so maximizing one claw is an advantage.

Bigger claws win fights, so a crab with one massive claw still beats another male with two equal-sized but smaller claws in a duel. Males attempt to rip the claw off their rivals, because essentially it denudes them and makes them far less attractive to females. Winning fights and mating with females is important to land crab males.

The next appendages are four pairs of walking legs, which, as you may have guessed, are used for walking but also for digging their extensive burrows. These burrows go down to water level and sometimes interconnect to other burrows, allowing for an escape route in treacherous times.

The Great Land Crab is edible, a tasty addition to West Indian stews. However, they are also one of the few animals that can eat the poisonous fruit of the Manchineel tree. Eating a crab that has feasted on some of these "death apples" (as Columbus referred to them) can cause ulcerations throughout the human digestive tract. So it's best to capture them alive and feed them a little corn or other vegetable scraps until they've processed the toxic fruit. Then you can add them to your delicious stew.

Just a short way down the road, you pass an area of recovering mangroves. Look closely at the ground to see hundreds of small, evenly spaced holes punctuating the mud. This time the openings are only about the size of a quarter. Wait for it. Finally a tiny crab with a disproportionately large claw, or chela, may emerge. These aren't baby land crabs; these are fiddler crabs.

The most common fiddler in the West Indies is Burger's (*Uca burgersi*) with the Caribbean Fiddler (*Uca rapax*) a close second. You can tell them apart by color. Burger's has red on the carapace and claw, while the Caribbean Fiddler has no red at all but a beautiful turquoise splotch between its stalked eyes. Again the huge claw signals amorous or aggressive intent.

If you haven't had enough of crabs, stop at Little Lameshur Beach to see if you can spot a sand-colored Ghost Crab running from the surf on the wet sand. The Ghost Crab is perhaps the most adorable crab on the island.

Even though you find all these different crabs in a small area, each one has a particular role in the environment. The land and fiddlers, both living on the mud flats, have partitioned their food requirements by size, while the ghost crab is specialized for life on sand. There are numerous other types crabs on the island: Mangrove Crabs patrol the mangroves and specialize in climbing the prop roots and branches of the trees. Hermit or Soldier Crabs scour the forest for debris. And we haven't even mentioned the various marine crabs living in the sea. Each crab has a niche. No two species can have the same niche, because one would eventually prevail over the other. Ecologists refer to this concept as Gause's Principle of Competitive Exclusion.

A rich habitat with multiple niches to fill creates a higher level of biological diversity. Having a lot of different species in an area is important for a stable food web. Most species eat more than one thing, so extra threads in the web mean more options. Think of it this way: imagine you are crossing a canyon on a rope suspension bridge. Would you like that bridge to have a lot of strands forming secure footholds every step of the way? Gaping holes are bad news for rope bridges and food webs.

The road continues past the beach and ends at the head of the Lameshur Bay Trail. From here, it's only about half a mile to walk to Europa Bay, which passes through a shady forested area. Huge mature Kapok and Tamarind trees are scattered in what looks to be a stand of similarly aged Genip trees. Genips are introduced and invasive; when you find them, you often find lots and lots of them. The area was used for grazing livestock in the not-too-distant past, so the large trees were probably left for shade while cattle and goats grazed the hillside.

A cluster of pinguin, also known as wild pineapple, grows near the trail. This thorny plant was used as natural fencing during the plantation era and is still used this way today. The flat dirt trail continues along under a natural archway of trees for a stint until the route inclines up a slight hill. A left turn on to the Europa Bay Trail takes you to the rocky shore of this rugged bay.

Cliffs edge the water to the north exposing jagged contours created by the silhouettes of bromeliads and cactus. As you look south, to the right, you'll see rocky outcroppings embracing the sea and holding the bay within. In the morning, the sun shines straight onto the white shore with its remains of broken and dried sea fans, pieces of sponges, fragments of coral, and sea urchin tests (outer skeletons).

Swimming is not advisable, but a walk along the water's edge will reveal a smattering of the animal diversity found within the waters of the bay. Looking from the tree line to the shore, you can tell how far up the water can reach during storms or surges. The empty shells of West Indian Top snails, nerites, limpets, clams, and other bivalves litter the rubble.

While they're alive, mollusks have a fleshy, slimy body that consists of two parts. The gooey part that sometimes hangs out of its shell is the head-foot that controls locomotion, eating, and sensory activity. The inner section, usually hidden deep inside the shell, is its visceral mass, which contains the organs for digestion and reproduction.

Today I found a Measled Cowrie that's as long as the palm of my hand. These creatures live deep in the sea; nevertheless, fish, rays, and sea stars discover them and eat their fleshy innards. The empty shell left behind is light and gets tossed by the waves and strewn onto the shore. This individual was an adult, indicated by its white spots, while its size reveals that it was probably a fully mature female. In fact, it's half an inch longer than typical specimens of this species.

She probably had many egg clutches that she laid in protected crevasses, where she stayed and brooded them until they hatched. After about three weeks, her young, free-swimming snail babies would emerge and be carried off in the ocean currents to inhabit new areas. The juvenile snails have a fragile, incomplete shell at first, but as they grow, their mantle, which is a thin membranous hood of tissue over their body, secretes the shell-building material and a thicker, more substantial outer home encases their vulnerable insides. In three months, they look like small adults, though without spots. After seven months, they mature enough to mate and have their own offspring.

Low tide exposes a thin black band of wet rocks where living creatures struggle between the force of the waves and the drying heat of the sun. Hundreds of periwinkles inside their cone-shaped spiral shells can be found clinging to the damp boulders, along with primitive-looking chitons. Chitons are another type of mollusk, perhaps the original prototype because they are associated with geologic eras as far back as the Paleozoic.

Chitons look like elongated ovals, bilaterally symmetrical, with eight shelly plates embedded on their dorsal surface. Their underside reveals a mouth, gills, and a long foot that secretes a substance more adhesive than most glue. At night, chitons slide along, scouring algae off stones. Males expel sperm directly into the water, some of which finds its way into females to fertilize eggs. A few species of chitons are ovoviviparous, meaning the female allows the eggs to develop inside her, appearing to give birth to live young. For most types, however, the eggs are laid singly or sometimes in long jelly-like strings. An adult female will lay thousands of eggs in her lifetime, because most of them end up as food for an assortment of marine creatures. If one of the tiny free-floating eggs can survive to become a rock-clinging adult, its biggest threat then becomes desiccation.

The number of individual animals residing within the cracks and crevasses of this beach reaches in the millions, but the number of species is probably only a dozen or two. It's a specialized existence, and only critters that have been selected through time and evolution have adapted to the alternating water levels and pounding force of the ocean. The unrelenting crashing of the waves fails to dislodge the snails and chitons, and even in this harsh environment, life endures, niches are populated, and evolution continues.

CHAPTER 8

The Dock

This night brings a moonless, cloudy sky, and I could not be more excited. We're at the VIERS lab—several adults and about twenty kids—about to walk on to the dock. My friend and fellow educator, Nancy, instructs the kids to turn off their flashlights to let their eyes adjust to the dark before we walk any farther toward the view of the water.

We're hoping to see bioluminescence tonight. The timing is about right, with the full moon still two and a half weeks away. There are no yachts in Greater Lameshur Bay this July night, and the only light shines from the security lamps at the lab.

At first the kids don't see it. They expect it to look like the images they've seen online with people kayaking in a glowing blue halo. It's much more subtle. The glow forms a smattering of sparkling green shooting stars in the sea. Some kids see it and some miss it.

After a while, sitting on the edge of the dock with legs hanging down, someone's feet splash the water, and it happens. The kids come to realize that the more you disturb the water, the more the light flashes. A frenzy of splashing feet reveals even more blue-green radiance, and it starts to connect.

This all makes sense, because the organisms that create the light do so as a means of defense. When they feel the turbulence of another being getting too close to them, they set off a chemical reaction within their single-celled bodies to create a distraction, a burst of light. These creatures are small but not invisible; in fact, anything with eyes can see them. Daytime is a very dangerous time to cruise the water column looking for yummy phytoplankton, but fortunately for these particular dinoflagellates, hunting phytoplankton in the dark is their specialty.

So while their phytoplankton prey take in the sunlight during the day, they descend down the water column, where light is more limited and visibility hindered. In the evening, as the newly sugared-up phytoplankton linger on the ocean's surface, filled up from the day's photosynthesizing, basically on pause until the sun comes up again, a hungry crowd of bioluminescent dinoflagellates floats upward, eager to engulf their tiny autotrophic prey.

The only problem is that as dinoflagellates become more numerous, they attract the attention of copepods and tiny fish that, in turn, love to dine on *them*. What's a dinoflagellate to do? Some of these amazing, colorless, unicellular creatures use spines, toxins, armor, or speed to elude would-be predators, while others use the flash-of-light-in-your-face trick.

If you can't imagine that as an effective escape strategy, I challenge you and some friends to shut yourselves up in a very dark hallway and play a game of tag. You're it, and all you have to do is tag one of your friends. But they have really awesome flashlights, like the kind police use, except they turn on only for a second at a time.

You zero in on one of your friends. You don't know if it's Caleb or Jenn or Olivia, but you're about to tag her or him, and *click*, you just got a blinding flash of light in your eyes. Chances are you didn't tag your friend, and for a few precious seconds you're disoriented and maybe even a little mad. Where *did* Jenn go? This game actually sounds fun to me, but I don't recommend it for real, because you could do some serious damage to people's retinas shining a police light in their eyes this way.

Okay, so we agree that it's effective. How does it happen? The process is actually more common in nature than you might imagine. Think fireflies, glowworms, squid, and anglerfish. Most organisms that use bioluminescence actually conduct the same chemical reaction in special vacuoles inside their cells to achieve the light blast. Luciferin is the light-emitting pigment, but turning on the light requires energy, oxygen, and a special enzyme called Luciferase (and sometimes additional cofactors like $Mg2+$).

There are actually a few other mechanisms that can create biological light, but this is how the ones in St. John and other parts of the Caribbean manage it. Each individual projects only a momentary flash, yet the light seems prolonged because so many individuals are involved. Dinoflagellates live a short life but can reproduce quickly when conditions are right, creating a bloom; think red tide or the green slime of algae that can cover a pond.

A bioluminescent bloom is beautiful, though a bit of a double-edged sword for the dinoflagellates, because as they become more numerous and the light becomes more prevalent, they attract even more of their predators. As smaller prey attract slightly larger predators, and then still larger predators, and so on, the situation in the water gets very interesting.

Collecting plankton with a net reveals a multitude of shapes and sizes from the unseen to the unbelievably huge. The term *plankton* quite literally includes all organisms that float adrift in water. So anything that can't swim against the current could be defined as plankton, even if it's as enormous as a jellyfish. So many kinds of organisms wander amid the ocean currents that plankton are characterized by their size and their functional group—that is, whether or not they photosynthesize, ingest, or absorb their food.

Ninety-five percent of life in the ocean is plankton, and the bottom line is that, without plankton, the food web of the ocean would collapse. Some plankton are eaten directly, but even when they aren't ingested, eventually they die or eliminate wastes, and in so doing create something referred to as marine snow. Marine snow gently sinks to the ocean floor and provides nutrients for burrowing decomposers that comprise the bottom tier of the substrate food web. These organisms process biological material, releasing more nutrients into the sediment and remineralizing organic matter in the water column. And so the cycle continues.

The VIERS dock holds a fascination for me in the daylight too. The posts supporting the planks of the dock serve as an attachment site for barnacles, oysters, hydroids, Feather Dusters, and even anemones. Banded Coral Shrimp, along with Arrow Crabs, creep up and down the vertical terrain of the wooden pillars and pick off edible morsels. The occasional boat or snorkeler stirs the sediments at the bottom, providing a surge of organic particles to swirl around the dock, sustaining the filter feeders and zooplankton. It seems there is always a school of Silversides hanging out nearby, capitalizing on the daily plankton migration, which in turn attracts a solitary Great Barracuda to loiter under the dock. Turning over rocks (and later gently replacing them) reveals black brittle stars, bristle worms (remember not to touch them, or you could get stung), mollusks, and even sea cucumbers.

One year an octopus occupied a space under a few rocks near the dock. His (or her) midden, which was simply a heap of empty bivalve shells in front of his tiny cave, revealed his presence. The spot was so shallow you could lie on your stomach with your head extending from the side of the dock and watch him meticulously make his way to the pilings, pull an oyster from the wood, take it back to his hiding place, and within minutes discard the empty shell.

Whenever I snorkel at the VIERS dock—or any dock, for that matter—I marvel at all the creatures living there. One day maybe I'll find a sea horse.

Day Four

*The sea is as near
as we come
to another world.*
Anne Stevenson

Brown Pelican

CHAPTER 9

Salt Pond Bay

If you decide to go to Salt Pond Bay, and I insist that you do, plan on hiking. Yes, the beach is breathtaking, but the trek up to the top of Ram Head is the most satisfying hike up to a view that you'll find on St. John.

Walking along the water to the end of the beach and saving my swim for after my ramble, I find the beginning of the trailhead. I prefer to do it early in the morning, because the southern exposed peninsula gets baking hot through the day, and it's just not as much fun if you're on the verge of heat stroke. Bring water (lots) and a little snack to nibble on when you reach the summit. Linger. Bring a sketchbook and draw. Watch for a turtle poking its head out of the sea and Frigate birds riding the wind at eye level.

You'll observe pelicans and terns soaring, but you might also spot a pair of Ground Doves. These gentle birds coo and waddle among the Turk's Cap Cactus, looking for the pink fruits that drop from the red fez on top of the barrel-shaped plant. Some people mistake these birds for baby Mourning Doves, because they look like a miniature version, but the Ground Dove is a separate species. Sometimes Ground Doves make their nest inside a hollowed out Turk's Cap. It's a safe haven if the entry is small enough, and any advantage is important to birds that nest low to the ground, especially with mongooses and cats in the neighborhood. On your way back, make a cairn on the blue cobble beach, then head for the sandy beach for your swim and snorkel.

I saw my first Peacock Flounder in Salt Pond Bay. The sun was brilliant, and I was just dunking my head under the water when I caught a glimpse of movement out of the corner of my eye. At first I couldn't tell what it was; it looked like sand moving. But as I watched, the sea floor transformed from mottled light browns to reveal an olive-colored flat fish with striking blue rings and splotches. The transformation took a matter of ten seconds. I'm not sure why it decided to unveil itself, but the effect on me was profound. I just watched and marveled while it lifted itself off the bottom and swam away in a kind of undulating rhythm.

When I came to my senses, I followed, but it had swum—no, pulsed—to a rock outcropping, already burrowing into the sand. The fish, a Peacock Flounder, sometimes referred to as Flower Flounder or Plate Fish, was flicking sand on top of itself with its pectoral fin and tail, changing its color back to mottled browns.

Researchers have studied the Peacock Flounder's ability to achieve cryptic coloration; it all comes down to visual cues detected by both of its eyes. It turns out they're really bad at it if one eye is covered with sand. But I want to know why they would want to be bright—ever. I can understand why the flounder would want to be the sandy color of the ocean bottom, but why have those vibrant blues at all? My guess is that it's a sex thing. Demonstrating one's ability for extreme color-changing just might be foreplay, a signal to other Peacock Flounders that it's time to party. At the very least, accumulating all the coenzymes required for intense color changes, along with the neural capacity to do it well, represents a high level of fitness for an individual Peacock Flounder hoping to score.

The body of an adult flounder is a strange twist of fate. As a juvenile, it appears rather normal, with eyes on each side of its bilaterally symmetrical body. As it grows into an adult, the right eye begins to change and move upward toward the top of its head until it's clearly on the left side of its body. The left pectoral fin grows significantly larger than the right, its swim bladder degenerates, and the pigment cells on the left side become more numerous and pronounced.

What we think of as the top and bottom of the fish actually isn't. The right side of the flounder becomes the blind side, with no eye, a stubby pectoral fin, and bland pigmentation. What we see as the top of the flounder is actually its left side. This metamorphosis from free-swimming larva to bottom-dwelling adult seems inconvenient to the point of heroism. Mutation or adaptation, I guess it's what you make of it. What may have been one glitch after another worked out eventually, and the strange Picasso-esque fish is a peculiar beauty to behold.

Other fish achieve a bottom-dwelling existence without the developmental shenanigans exhibited by the Peacock Flounder. Southern Stingrays and Nurse Sharks have a similar bottom-dwelling, functional niche. Both rays and Nurse Sharks have a cartilaginous skeleton that makes them extremely flexible, though the ray has a more pancake shape and a greatly elongated tail. The ray's mouth is on its underside, and though it can crack open mollusks and crabs, it's not in a position to use the teeth defensively.

Hold on, though, because on the end of its long tail, the stingray has a jagged barb. When threatened, the stingray holds its tail over its head like a scorpion and drives the barb into its opponent. To avoid getting poked by a stingray barb, shuffle your feet if you're walking in sea grass beds. If you're snorkeling, try not to sneak up on stingrays. This is generally good advice when it comes to any fish bigger than your head or longer than your arm. But don't worry; it's not easy to be stealthier than a sea creature in the water.

Southern Stingrays and Nurse Sharks are both nocturnal feeders and hang out on the sea bottom during the day. The stingray often burrows under the sand, while the shark likes to huddle in the spaces beside or under rocks. Seeing either of these species in Salt Pond Bay is likely but shouldn't be cause for alarm. They almost never pay any attention to divers or snorkelers and will behave as if you're not there—that is, unless you decide to harass them, so don't do that, for your own sake and because it's mean.

As you snorkel, try to notice all the little fish that live on the surface of the corals and rocks. Blennies and gobies, which are among the smallest and most numerous species of fish on reefs, are masters of the microniche. Their tiny size and interesting antics also make them among the most sought-after species for home aquariums. I prefer to see them in their natural habitat, but snorkeling in the ocean is distracting, because there's so much to see, so many places to look, and a lot of bigger things to look at.

Focus on a small area. Choose a spot that seems to have some diversity of texture and color, and you'll find that the longer you look, the more you'll see. Be patient. That Red-Lipped Blenny isn't going to pop its head out of its crevasse the instant you show up. Give it a few minutes. While you're waiting, listen. The snapping and crackling noises are the sounds of jaws munching and claws shutting. Try putting one finger on a bare rock to help steady yourself in place, allowing your body to flow back and forth with the waves. Remember, there is no race, no mandatory distance to cover, and you have arrived at your destination.

CHAPTER 10

Drunk Bay

If you have only one beach day in St. John and you need amenities like toilets, a snack bar, showers, and an entry fee, by all means check out Trunk Bay. The underwater snorkeling trail there is nifty, and the beach is beautiful. It's the most photographed beach on St. John, which is code for "most visited by cruise ship passengers." Enough said.

On the other hand, Drunk Bay (not to be confused with Trunk Bay) is a short walk from the beach at Salt Pond Bay. Perhaps they call it this because you'd have to be drunk to think this would be a good place to swim. Drunk Bay faces Norman Island to the east. From there, if you had a string, you could unroll it all the way across the Atlantic to Africa before you'd hit land. Suffice it to say that a lot of flotsam washes up on the cobble beach at Drunk Bay.

What does one do with hunks of coral, fragments of boats, strands of seaweed, bits of rope, and pieces of fish traps washed ashore? Make art, of course! Fanciful sculptures of giraffes, women, and anatomically correct pirates can be found on the rocky shores of Drunk Bay. The art scene here is ever changing, with new visitors adding more and storms taking out the existing. Rearranging items to make a coral sculpture is borderline rule-breaking in the National Park, so embrace your inner hooligan and make something too. Some laws of etiquette do apply however: never take a piece from one sculpture to make your own, never use anything living, and take only trash from the beach, because it's a national park and you're suppose leave things as they were.

Along the path between Drunk Bay and the beach at Salt Pond Bay, you'll pass the salt pond for which the bay is named. Occasionally, when conditions are right, as when it's windy, hot, sunny, and hasn't rained in a while, salt gathers on the edges of the pond. The salt collected contains all the minerals of the ocean. I recommend two cups in a warm bath, or you could use a little of it on your food.

If you look closely into the pond, you'll see some tiny organisms that look almost pink. These are adult Brine Shrimp, a critical food source for a good number of sea birds, bats, crabs, and other animal visitors to the salt pond. In the pond, where the salinity can be high, only organisms that can withstand this extreme environment can live. Because dried eggs of Brine Shrimp can remain viable for up to two years, they're used extensively in aquaculture. The eggs of this tiny creature are intriguing because it seems that no matter what you do, whether you heat, desiccate, freeze, or violently shake them, they still hatch. However, taking them into space and exposing them to cosmic rays apparently causes death during development. (I'm not kidding. These eggs have actually traveled to the moon and back.)

Not too far from this spot, Hermit Crabs (*Ceonobita clypeatus*), a distant cousin of the Brine Shrimp, perform one of the most spectacular mating events of the year. Locally known as Soldier Crabs, this fist-sized arthropod hangs out in and around wet places among the roots or even branches of trees. Mostly they eat debris, which can include iguana poop, rotting fruit, and soft wood, but in some places where people gather, they also eat scrambled eggs and old cheese.

Their shell is actually a borrowed shell and not an exoskeleton (although they do have one of those too). They commandeer a shell from a mollusk, such as the West Indian Topshell or other sea snail, to use as protection because their backsides are rather vulnerable. The number of suitable shells available limits the size of their population, because only those individuals with an intact shell that covers their squishy parts can survive an attack from a Pearly Eyed Thrasher or other hungry predator.

Every summer, Soldier Crabs migrate from their terrestrial homes in the hills and forests. They gather in one spot near the water and wait for all of their brethren to arrive. Males and females mate just before the August full moon. At a certain time that only they know, they all make a break for the beach. The females need to deposit their eggs in the sea, though they need to be careful, because they can't swim. It's not clear if all the crabs that come to the beach are females or if the males accompany them, yet one thing is for sure: it's a dangerous time.

A very cool video shot by island photographer Steve Simonsen captures the massive migration of Soldier Crabs at Nanny Point (https://vimeo. com/48466065). You should definitely check it out. When this many crabs gather, pelicans and terns are going to notice. So between competing for the best shell and avoiding becoming lunch, the sense of urgency for the females to get those eggs into the ocean is high.

You might be thinking, *Why do that? Why draw attention to yourselves that way?* Perhaps if one or two females at a time were to sneak down to the beach, not as many predators would be alerted to the action. That's probably true. But when they are, and they will be, then it becomes a game of sit and wait for the food to walk by. If you all go down as a hoard, however, individual chances become better. Think of it as winning the lottery—the bad kind though, as in the *Hunger Games*. The more crabs the better the odds for each one. The same goes for depositing the eggs. By depositing millions and millions of eggs in the sea all at once, some of them are bound to succeed.

This scenario illustrates an important concept that eludes humans. A critical minimum number of individuals are needed to sustain a population. It's not sufficient to have some Hermit Crabs or a few Nassau Groupers or a couple of Leatherback Sea Turtles. There has to be an adequate number of individuals to satiate the predators, *plus* more to survive long enough to contribute offspring to the next generation. Most of the eggs deposited will never be adult crabs. But they are still incredibly valuable. Those eggs turn out to be food for so many other species, for at every different stage of their development, they become another thread in the food web of the sea.

Day Five

The cure for anything is salt water:
sweat, tears or the sea.
Isak Dinesen

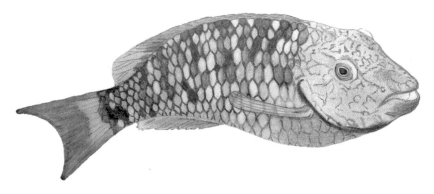

Stoplight Parrotfiish

CHAPTER 11

Haulover Bay

The East End of St. John begins just after Skinny Legs, more or less. The road winds, climbs, and dips. In some parts you might be tempted to honk your horn to let a vehicle coming from the other direction know you're heading down the hairpin hill. Here's where driving on the left, if it's not your usual road rule, gets hairy. In many sections there doesn't seem to be enough room for two cars, so you stay sort of in the middle. As you round a bend and discover an oncoming car, your instinct is to veer right, which is wrong. Hug the left side of the road at all the times when driving in St. John. Also, learn to love low gears, because riding the brake pedal will just be bad news—eventually.

On the way to Haulover Bay in St. John, views of Tortola seem so close it's hard to believe there are international waters between the two islands. The closeness of these two landmasses creates a surge in the current that makes snorkeling in this northern bay of the East End dangerous when the wind and the waves are too strong. On the other hand, when conditions are good, it's fantastic!

The National Park Service has marked the area from the road nicely, and there are parking spaces, though not many, that keep the jeeps off the pavement. The short trail to the north-facing bay might have the highest density of mosquitos on the island. (And I'm only exaggerating a little. Once I got twenty-six mosquito bites in five minutes on this trail.) The path emerges on a rocky beach strewn with Sargasso Weed that's just wide enough to set your stuff down on.

The coral here is really close to the shore, so I put my mask on at the water's edge and immediately place my face in the water to maneuver around without touching the living structures before me. The combination of soft coral, like sea fans, sea whips, and sea plumes, along with hard, reef-building corals like Brain, Star, and Finger Coral, is as diverse as it gets so close to the shore. Typically you'd have to take a boat to places much farther out to encounter this kind of community.

This is the New York City of shoreline snorkeling. Even the fish seem busy and more hurried than in other places. Within minutes, I see four different species of parrotfish and a multitude of phases of each. There are damselfish, wrasses, gobies, grunts, and snappers. The various classes of age and gender make them challenging to identify for snorkelers just starting out.

Like birds, many fish are sexually dimorphic, which just means that the males and the females look different. Consider birds, like the ones that might visit a bird feeder; these are mainly of the passerine variety. Baby passerines look nothing like their adult parents, but once a bird fledges from the nest and starts flying around on its own, it's difficult to tell a young one from an older individual of the same species. Plus, you can count on all Blue Jays, American Robins, Black-capped Chickadees, etc., to look the same.

Unlike birds, though, fish vary in color and size within species. Take something as straightforward as a Blue Tang. Tangs are easy to identify— most of the time. If you see a thin-bodied blue fish with a roundish profile, you can assume that it's a Blue Tang, and you may be correct. But you might have a Doctor Fish or Ocean Surgeonfish. All three of these species have a spine like a switchblade at the base of their tails. Because that spine has been compared to a doctor's scalpel, we can understand why all three of these species are in the family referred to as the Surgeon Fishes (*Acanthuridae*).

All of the individuals of this family can also change color to suit their environment, mood, age, or reproductive desires. They can be powder blue or a deep sapphire blue. They can look greenish brown when hovering over grass beds. They can look from pale or dark to nearly black. Juveniles can be completely yellow or have just a yellow tail. Surgeon Fish might aggregate in mixed schools or forage alone. Their shape tells you it's one of the Surgeon Fish; the presence of bars, lack of bars, or horizontal striping helps determine which species you have; color is just the start.

In addition to the marauding tangs, busy parrotfish dart and race about, keeping their tube-shaped bodies straight while pumping their pectoral fins. Occasionally, you'll find one motionless while Cleaning Gobies clean its body for ectoparasites. Sometimes it looks like they're just taking a rest, aligning next to a sea fan or hovering within the embracing arms of an Elkhorn Coral.

At night, a parrotfish might secrete a membrane that it uses as a sleeping bag. Scientists think it keeps their scent hidden but might also conceal their electromagnetic pulses that sharks use to detect prey. In the morning, they don't roll up their bag; they simply eat it as their first meal of the day.

Parrotfish and wrasses are closely related species, found commonly around reefs and in particular abundance here at Haulover Bay. Parrotfish have a thick body. Between their gills and tail, their scales appear highly visible, as though they've been outlined with a marker. Parrotfish can be colorful with blues, greens, pinks, yellows, reds, and whites, but it's their fused front teeth that give them their name. Chomping and scraping coral, which you can actually hear underwater, they shape and prune the reef with their mouths. Like tangs and damselfish, they're herbivores.

But hey, why are they eating the coral if coral are animals? Parrotfish are after the *Zooxanthellae* that are the symbiotic residents inside the coral polyps. They eat other forms of algae and plant life too, which is good for the coral, because the free-living algae block the sunlight. Although the corals themselves don't need sunlight, their resident *Zooxanthellae* do; ample light means lots of photosynthesis. Photosynthesis turns water (H_2O) and carbon dioxide (CO_2) into sugar (CH_2O) and oxygen. Fish need oxygen, and the Zooxanthellae provide the coral with their excess sugar for energy.

An additional benefit of the *Zooxanthellae* is that through their physiological processes the acid level inside the coral polyps is greatly reduced, which is super important if you're an organism that wants to lay down a layer of calcium carbonate for structural support. Hard corals like

Brain and Star Coral don't just host their *Zooxanthellae* for a sugar high; they need them to build the reefs.

So while the relationships between the coral, their *Zooxanthellae*, and the parrotfish can be complex, the organization within the parrotfish species can also be complicated. Take, for instance, one species, the Stoplight Parrotfish. The juvenile stage can last for up to five years, with males and females that look similar. They have a dark reddish body with some brown or green, as well as three rows of bright white spots.

If a Stoplight Parrotfish is born male, it will remain male throughout its life. These are primary males and will often mate as a group, spawning with one or more females present. However, as a female matures, she might change her sex to male—and is then referred to as a super male or terminal male. This can happen even if she has mated as a female, but usually happens when the density of primary males is low.

While primary males retain the red and gray-green scale coloration, a terminal male becomes a beautiful green, blue, and yellow version of the Stoplight Parrotfish. Terminal males tend to keep a harem of females, though they court and mate with only one of the females. If a terminal male meets his demise, the remaining females will begin to change sex. Usually the largest female changes into the new terminal male first, then begins producing a male pheromone that halts the sex change in all the other females nearby.

Gender isn't always determined by chromosomes; for some animals environmental conditions influence the sex of individuals. In crocodiles and sea turtles, the temperature of the eggs during development determines gender. True hermaphrodites—individuals with both sets of sex organs—are more common in snails, worms, and tunicates, though gender permanence is not a hard-and-fast rule for many vertebrate species. Sequential hermaphrodites—animals that start out one sex and change to the opposite sex—include sex-changing clown fish that turn from male to female (yes, Nemo could eventually become a female), while species like Cleaner Wrasses turn from female to male. To my knowledge there has never been a report of a group of primary male Stoplight Parrotfish ganging up on and attacking a terminal male.

CHAPTER 12

Hurricane Hole

From the road, mangroves look like a muddy, buggy tangle of roots and branches—in other words, completely uninviting to most people. This is precisely why they're nutritious, productive areas teaming with wildlife. Birds often nest in mangroves because they're more inaccessible to terrestrial predators than open areas. Plus, the trees buzz with flies, which attract spiders, crabs, and lizards, which themselves are also good food. Even frogs will climb on the smooth brown bark of white and black mangroves, peeping their calls and snacking on mosquitos. The foliage casts shade, keeping the mud underneath cool from the hot sun. Water puddles become breeding pools for critters, and the poop from the terrestrial residents serves to add needed nitrogen, phosphorus, and other micronutrients to the mud.

The amazing adaptations that allow mangrove roots to exist in salty mud with almost no oxygen content, in the transition zone between land and sea, salt and freshwater, are nothing short of spectacular. In fact, people have taken a page out of the mangrove handbook and modeled our desalination plants to work in the same way as their cells work to extrude salt and stay hydrated.

Their extensive root systems stabilize the trees in the shifting conditions that come with living in mud, dealing with the influx of rain from storms and wave action from hurricanes. Buffering the land from the ocean and protecting the sea from the runoff from roads is a valuable ecological service. Protecting mangroves from developers is more important than most people realize.

If you approach mangroves from the sea, with a snorkel and mask, you'll be rewarded with a window into a nursery of the reefs. Tiny, colorful, juvenile fish flitter between the arched roots of red mangroves that are patrolled by baby Barracudas, Schoolmasters, and Bar Jacks. Schools of Silversides linger near the roots with an occasional Butterfly Fish or Trunkfish interrupting the scene. Brightly hued sponges encrust the branches and clarify the water around the roots so that it's often clearer than the bay beyond.

In St. John, four bays—Borck Bay, Princess Bay, Otter Creek, and Water Creek—are collectively known as Hurricane Hole—aptly named because in the past, boats would converge in this area to ride out storms. Vessels were sheltered from the winds by the shape of the land around the bays, benefiting also from the mangroves' ability to absorb the onslaught of high storm water. The mangroves found within Hurricane Hole are, for the most part, protected by the US National Park as part of the Virgin Islands Coral Reef National Monument. Now it's no longer a haven for boats seeking shelter but a refuge for juvenile fish, Queen Conch, Spiny Lobster, and corals.

Of the forty-five species of corals found in the entire Virgin Islands Coral Reef National Monument, thirty are found in Hurricane Hole. In addition, the coral here are among the healthiest specimens in the park. Here, the coral has evaded the incidences of warming that have left corals in other parts of the Caribbean bleached and diseased. For most of the day, parts of the mangroves are shaded and remain comfortably cool even in shallow areas.

Snorkeling on the fringe of the mangroves is like looking through the glass of an aquarium, except it's real life. Calmly and carefully floating along the edge of the mangroves, you have access to view the corals and sponges that have spilled out. Looking into the roots, you'll discover the shy individuals that are too small to venture into the open sea.

This is a special place, a place we need to treat with care, so please don't wear your fins. If you're worried about staying afloat, use a noodle or a snorkel vest. Avoid touching anything with your hands or feet. Explore the adjacent sea grass beds, where you might find a party of Pin Cushion

Sea Stars or an Upside Down Jellyfish. Try to locate a spot where there are a lot of different substrates like corals, Rope Sponge, sea grasses, and rock. Linger there, remembering that the more you look, the more you'll see.

In Otter and Water Creeks (which are actually bays), it's easy to find individual coral heads. You can get a nice look at the structure of the skeleton and the form the colony takes as the polyps grow and multiply. Each species of coral has a characteristic growth pattern; some take shape as mounds, like Brain Coral; balls, like Star Coral; or antlers, like Staghorn Coral.

A calcium carbonate skeleton is secreted from the live, fleshy polyps. As it grows and dies, the hard surface remaining is the perfect substrate for baby polyps, which are formed via budding. In time, you have the distinguishing forms that appear in the guidebooks. Most of the coral polyps on an individual mound or pillar are genetic clones of one another. But coral can reproduce sexually as well, which is how corals disperse their progeny to faraway places.

Two modes of sexual reproduction are used by the majority of stony corals. The broadcast spawners produce eggs and sperm in their polyps and release them at the same time during only a few nights per year. Each species has its own unique timing, but it's synchronized so that all individuals of that species release their gametes on the same nights, usually during a full moon. (Romantic, I know!) The gametes float to the surface of the ocean and intermingle. Sperm fertilizes eggs while fish and zooplankton eat as many gametes as they possibly can.

Only a tiny percentage of the remaining zygotes (fertilized eggs) go on to develop into an adult polyp. The odds against the offspring of broadcast spawners is great, hence, the enormous number of gametes produced. Once fertilized, a tiny zygote still needs to grow, develop, and settle on a hard surface to begin the long, slow process of forming a colony.

The other strategy used by stony corals is brooding. Only about 25 percent of coral species use this method; it's most successful where healthy colonies of corals already exist. In this case, colonies of polyps release only sperm. These male gametes float upward and get churned in the waves. In time, the sperm takes in seawater and begins to sink; if it's lucky enough to encounter a female polyp of the same species, it will be taken in, similar to how a polyp might ingest plankton.

Inside the body of the polyp, the sperm fertilizes an egg. The egg grows, still inside the adult polyp, and when it becomes a planula, ready to begin life on its own, it's released through the oral opening, typically settling close to the parent colony. Thinking about the chances of survival of a typical coral sperm—or human or frog sperm for that matter—it's a wonder that anything reproduces at all. Such is the miracle of life.

Even though Hurricane Hole is only one community, its impact on coral in the entire Caribbean may be significant. The thirty species that live here continue to grow colonies, contributing to the recruitment of corals in other areas of St. John and possibly beyond.

To some, it may be a financial hardship that boats have to weather hurricanes in a less protected bay. Storms can and do pose a hazard to people and property. As the number of boats increases and the number of healthy corals decreases, sacrifices have to be made. People enjoy the option to buy insurance, but what protection do corals have against extinction? For many species of corals, the only indemnity is a refuge known as Hurricane Hole.

Day Six

The human brain now holds the key
to our future.
We have to recall the image
of the planet from outer space:
a single entity
in which air, water, and continents
are interconnected.
David Suzuki

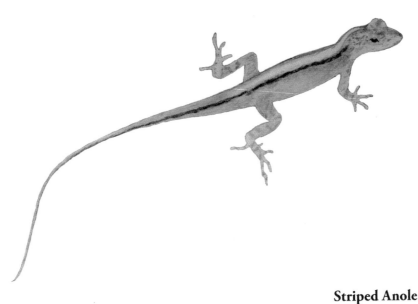

Striped Anole

CHAPTER 13

To the Petroglyphs and Back

Once again I find myself on the Lameshur Bay Trail, this time heading for the petroglyphs. A petroglyph is a rock carving, while a petrograph or pictograph is an image drawn or painted on rock. In St. John, there's a place where water falls from a high cliff during the rainy season, leaving a pool in a rock basin for most of the year. It's one of the few places where fresh surface water exists on the island; in ancient times, it would have been a special, even sacred, place.

On one side, a slab of boulder borders the pool. Viewed from the other side, carved symbols are visible both in the rock itself and also as a reflection. Taino Indians, which are perhaps the original inhabitants of St. John, might have considered this location an entrance to the other world—the place where their deceased ancestors lived.

It's unclear what these symbols mean, though Ken Wild, the chief archeologist at the US Virgin Islands National Park, offers a detailed thesis on the subject at the following website: www.friendsvinp.org/documents/Petro0204.pdf. Those interested in early culture on the island are encouraged to check it out.

In addition to tourists, many creatures visit this pool, including frogs and dragonflies, which deposit their eggs. I myself have seen crayfish, fish, and various water bugs, while bats have also been observed at the pool at night. It's a wonderful place to sit and ponder what life must have been like on the island before air-conditioning, sunscreen, and quick-dry clothing.

I first noticed how many species of pigeon and doves there were on St. John during a visit to the petroglyphs. In one day, I saw two Common Ground Doves waddling along on the Lameshur Bay Trail, while a few yards away I watch a Bridled Quail Dove bobbing its tail on a skinny branch as it voiced its mournful coo. Minutes later I came upon a Scaly-naped Pigeon climbing on a vine that hung from a tree. The vine was loaded with pink blossoms, and I couldn't tell if the pigeon was eating the flowers or insects in the buds.

When I arrived at the petroglyphs that day, three Zenaida Doves were rummaging around in the leaf litter at the base of the hill. Later, near the ruins at Reef Bay, I noticed a White-winged Dove that looked remarkably like the ubiquitous Mourning Dove, except for the white crescent that flanks its wing. There really is no scientific difference between a pigeon and a dove, for the family *Columbidae* includes birds with both names. Generally doves are smaller and associated with peace; what people would call a pigeon in a city park is called a Rock Dove by bird watchers.

Anoles, the small lizards you see jumping from tree to tree or scurrying over rocks, are also prevalent on St. John. You might notice them trying to act tough, by doing push-ups to impress females. It also lets other anoles know that they have been seen and they'd better get going. Anoles don't like to share their tree with other anoles.

Males also extend their dewlap—a colorful flap of skin under their chin—to indicate how sexy they are to females. A brightly colored dewlap is like a little neon sign that says, "I'm beautiful and a highly efficient forager! Don't you want your babies to be like me?" A dewlap is ingenious because an anole can wave it when he wants to be noticed but tuck it close to his chin when he wants to hide.

At best guess, there are 138 different species residing on all the Caribbean islands. This speciation began around fifty million years ago when the ancestral species first colonized four of the Greater Antillean Islands (Cuba, Hispaniola, Jamaica, Puerto Rico). Because the islands are not too distant from each other, individual anoles would show up on additional islands, floating on branches during a storm or by other means.

Once on a new island, the anoles would adapt and diverge from the parent group. On the larger islands, a form of evolution referred to as adaptive radiation occurred because there were lots of empty niches to fill. However, because conditions and habitats on the various islands can be similar, there appear to be predictable ecomorphs on some of the larger islands, according to where they live. (Ecomorphs, in this situation, are individuals that look similar because they live in similar habitats but have evolved independently on each island.)

In 2013, the journal *Science* published an article on this incidence of convergent evolution. D. Luke Mahler and his colleagues contend that anoles living in tree canopy or in grasslands tend to be green. By living in a habitat where being bright green is an advantage, lizards evolved to be bright green.

But even more remarkable than just color is that many of the similar species also evolved similar-sized crests or tail length in comparable habitats. Mahler and his colleagues found that this happened consistently in the Caribbean islands for species living in the tree canopy, on the ground, on tree trunks, and on twigs. Evolution in these habitats had a predictable outcome, which was a result of similar selective pressures from the environment on individuals. Thus the anoles on the different islands look similar despite being, in fact, different species. Of course, these lizards all come from the same common ancestor with a genetic plasticity that allowed for the adaptive modifications. It's exciting, though, to be a witness to further evidence for the theory of evolution by means of natural selection.

How many species of anoles are on St. John? I've identified at least four so far. The first and easiest to pick out are the Crested Anoles. These are the biggest and are brown or beige and have a prominent crest from their head to their tail. The Barred Anole looks like it has dashes along its back and is found on the trunks of trees or jumping on rocks in forested areas.

There is another species found in some of the same locations that has a conspicuous yellow stripe down the middle of its back. Let's refer to this one as the Striped Anole (because I haven't been able to make a scientific ID of it yet). And finally there's at least one species of Grass Anole that tends to be greenish beige, found mainly on leafy vegetation.

Are there genetic or morphological differences that can be seen and measured? For now, I am going to photograph, describe, and take notes on where I find anoles. I'm getting a few ideas for my next research project.

CHAPTER 14

Booby Rock

Walking past Little Lameshur Bay on the way back from the petroglyphs presents a tempting opportunity to snorkel out to Booby Rock. The waves beckon, and at this point, you need a shower or a swim, so the obvious choice is to wade in. Bring your waterproof camera, because with the sun high in the sky, underwater pictures have their best shot at brilliance; the abundance of shallow areas also allows you to get really close to your subject.

Booby Rock is always surrounded by interesting colors, whether it be from the fish or the sponges. Today a bright-red Encrusting Sponge is the backdrop for a juvenile Yellow-tailed Damselfish. This fish is jewel blue with a clear tail and electric blue spots all over its body. I've photographed this species dozens of times, and I will continue to take more, as none of my pictures ever captures the vivid glow of those spots. In my opinion, no photo, taken by any person, ever has.

Fish can be predictable. Each species has a favored place in the water column. It helps to use this information to make an identification. For instance, you won't find a damselfish swimming in open water. You will inevitably find a Dusky Damselfish near her or his rock garden. These fish are mainly algae eaters and prefer to stay near their food. For a small fish, they tend to be aggressive when guarding their turf. Take a few moments and just watch them. If a tang or Sergeant Major gets too close to its territory, he will dart toward it and shoo it away.

As adults, Dusky Damselfish are drab brown, but as juveniles they're blue with a splash of orange. The juveniles of all species of damselfish look different and are much more brightly colored than their adult counterparts. One might assume that this is to alleviate the competitiveness of adults against the young; scientific studies, however, have not supported this hypothesis. Perhaps it has nothing to do with the interaction between juveniles and adults within the same species. Blue Tangs are often aggressive toward other herbivores (but not each other) while juvenile tangs are bright blue and yellow. Could the bright blues of young damsels be an advantage when interacting with adult Tangs?

Instead of a Brown Booby sitting on the rock jutting out a few hundred meters from shore, a Royal Tern stands guard. The wind blows its black crown feathers aside, making it look like a bird with male pattern baldness. Its bright orange beak is set firmly closed, and its face is alert but relaxed. It surely knows there are some one hundred French Grunts just below, crowding the biggest Mutton Snapper I've ever seen. The Mutton Snapper is perhaps half the length of my body, way too big for the Royal Tern. But hey, a bird can dream. This huge white fish with its black spot is a sharp contrast to the smaller grunts, and as I look closer, I spy several Margates in the crowd.

Grunts, Margates, Grey Snappers, and even Mangrove Snappers often form mixed schools that seem like loitering masses during daylight hours. At night, they're a little more active, patrolling the sea for invertebrate prey: shrimp, crabs, and zooplankton. The grunts, named for the sound the teeth in their throat make when grinding together, are a middle-tier predator. They're also considered primary carnivores or carnivores that eat herbivores.

However, the levels of the trophic pyramid don't always align with typical or classical definitions, because many of the creatures in this food web are opportunistic—meaning, if an organism fits into your mouth and you can catch it, it will become your prey, regardless of its food choices. The presence of a lot of grunts suggests that there are a lot of invertebrate prey forming a stable base for larger predators like groupers or sharks.

Groupers tend to be shy during the day. You have to look under rocks and overhangs to find them. It's as if they don't trust being out in the open, because they understand that there are creatures like bigger groupers out there that eat fish. Just because a species normally hunts at night doesn't mean it won't take advantage of a situation.

My friend Lauren noticed an octopus one day, and in taking an interest in it caused the octopus to move to a more secure location. A Nassau Grouper, unseen by both Lauren and the octopus, was quietly observing the action. In an instant, as the octopus began to shift to a new spot, the Nassau Grouper darted out and swallowed the octopus whole. Opportunity. Lauren felt bad that her interest cost the octopus his or her life, but she admits that it was really cool to be a witness.

Like the Nassau Grouper that capitalized on the presence of Lauren, fish will often use each other to create opportunity. I watched a school of Blue Tangs move into damselfish territories and basically wreak havoc by devouring the algae that the damsels were so expertly harvesting. Too many tangs to save their crop, but the damsels surely tried by swimming frantically toward individual tangs, driving one away while another scooped in and snagged a bite. Meanwhile, a Trumpet Fish mingled among the tangs and clearly hoped to capitalize on the mayhem and suck in a few damselfish along the way. There was so much commotion, I couldn't tell if that Trumpet Fish was successful or not, but I imagine it's a winning strategy.

A wildlife moment can happen any time you snorkel, but don't expect it every time. The possibility of a sea turtle or a Spotted Eagle Ray exists any time you strap that mask to your face, but don't underestimate the calming beauty of a few Sergeant Majors. This is why I'll always choose to stop and snorkel at Booby Rock after a hike to the petroglyphs rather than going straight back to camp.

Day Seven

In every outthrust headland,
in every curving beach,
in every grain of sand
there is the story of the earth.
Rachel Carson

Smooth Trunkfish

CHAPTER 15

Waterlemon Cay

I was sitting on a rock near the Maho tree at the Leinster Bay trail entrance. Yellow blooms poked through the bright, heart-shaped, green leaves. With the turquoise sea and the warm breeze, I felt utterly calm. I was watching the "love bugs" (small black-and-red beetles) wiggle, shimmy, and climb all over each other. There were so many of them, perhaps a hundred or more, and I was entranced by their tiny movements. The love bugs were clearly motivated, for what I'll never know.

A man's voice broke through my serenity. "Hey, honey, grab the camera. I caught a sea cucumber!" My first thought was that, without legs, sea cucumbers can't exactly run away. They're not so much caught as found. The guy was excited and very pleased with himself, so I kept silent.

I became more amused and enamored with the couple as they examined the tubular creature that fit in the man's hand. The wife took at least twenty photographs. Just as I was thinking, *Wow, they've had that sea cucumber out of the water for a while*, they both shrieked. The sea cucumber had literally spilled its guts onto the guy's hand.

The surprise and disgust at the event caused the man to drop the sea cucumber, which of course is exactly what the sea cucumber wanted him to do. The whitish wormlike tangle of goo remained on his hand. I still remember the look on his face, partly because it remained there for about five minutes.

This is when I stood up and said, "It's okay. It's only a defensive response." I explained that, as a response to fear or being startled, sea cucumbers eject a portion of their respiratory organs known as cuvierian tubules. It's part of an autonomic process called evisceration, when a spontaneous tear in the cloaca allows them to expel these sticky threads. Sea cucumbers do it to surprise and entangle their would-be predators.

The guy still had that look on his face, and now his wife did too. This is when I mentioned that he might want to rinse the tubules off his hand, because sometimes they have a toxic secretion that can irritate skin. That's when his faced changed to an even *more* horrified look.

While he frantically splashed his hands in the water, I tried to salvage the situation by telling them how cool sea cucumbers are, that they eat a lot of detritus and dead things on the reef, and that they're an integral part of the food chain themselves. In fact, a lot of other organisms have symbiotic relationships with sea cucumbers. Take the Pearl Fish, for instance. Basically, it lives inside the sea cucumber's butt, coming out only at night.

This is when the couple started edging away from me toward the parking lot. I think my helpful commentary might actually have ruined sea cucumbers for them.

Luckily, my companions were ready to head out on our twenty-minute walk down the trail to the beach nearest to Waterlemon Cay. Yes, it's Water*lemon*, not Water*melon*, and no one seems to know why it's called that; it just is. This little island sits only a few hundred meters from the beach, and a swim that includes a sandy bottom, sea grass beds, and rock gardens leads to an elegant fringing reef that embraces the cay.

The diversity of life you can see in one hour is astounding, due in part to the diverse habitats found in this confined area. I swim counterclockwise around the tiny island when the ocean is calm. If the waves are rough, I stay within the bay and snorkel among the sea grasses. Pin Cushion Sea Stars, watchful Barracudas, octopus middens, and expensive yachts—this spot has something for everyone. Although there are never any guarantees, I've seen at least one sea turtle each time I've been here.

Four species of sea turtles might be spotted in St. John: the Green, Hawksbill, Leatherback, and very infrequently the Loggerhead. All four of these species are endangered. *Endangered* is a word that's used so often that we sometimes forget the significance of it. It means "likely to become extinct." Consider this when you have an urge to ride or to touch a sea turtle or follow it at a close distance. Although you might inadvertently swim toward a sea turtle, avoid chasing it. Not to mention that it's illegal to harass a sea turtle or marine mammal.

About 100 million years ago, animals that we would recognize as sea turtles, with their armored tank-like body and paddle-shaped limbs, swam in ocean waters. Most scientists believe that an asteroid struck the earth over 65 million years ago. While perhaps 85 percent of Earth's species perished, sea turtles made it through. Not every species of sea turtle and not even every family survived, but some did. The result was, though, that most species of sea turtle have very little genetic diversity. The extremely limited variation between individuals means that sea turtles are more likely to succumb to the same pathogens and pollutants.

Along with natural causes of mortality like disease and predation, sea turtles also have had to contend with beach development that eliminates their nesting sites. Something as seemingly benign as artificial lights near beaches lure young turtles to roads, parking lots, and sand dunes, where hatchlings die from desiccation. That's because, for most of their history on this planet, the moon was the brightest light in the night sky. Its reflection on the ocean cued newly emerged young to scurry toward the sea.

Sea turtles are long-lived creatures that take years, even decades, to get to the point of being mature enough to mate. A lot can happen in twenty years. Fishing nets and long-lines entangle adult turtles, and because like all reptiles they breathe air and not water, they can drown. Turtle exclusion devices on shrimp trawling nets have helped, but too many turtles continue to end up as bycatch on commercial fishing vessels. Although marine debris and plastic aren't food, sadly, they are still ingested by sea turtles. Turtles are hunted for their meat, shells, and eggs in many regions; for some people, it may be one of the only sources of protein.

On the other hand, through scientific research on the nesting habits of adult females and the successful hatching of eggs, people have begun to make real progress in conservation efforts. Because of programs that protect eggs from poachers as well as predators, the numbers of sea turtles in the Atlantic are actually on the rise. Breeding centers and educational activities have brought the plight of the sea turtle to the forefront, and many communities are recognizing the value in keeping sea turtle populations viable and stable, sparking sea turtle tourism. Bringing people in to see a nest of sea turtles hatch and then lumber to the sea has been found to bring in more money to the community than poached eggs.

Humans have an enormous capacity for empathy; getting more people to watch a tiny life wriggle free from a leathery egg just might help to save a species and a community.

CHAPTER 16

Departure

Whether you live here, are vacationing here, or simply are experiencing St. John through the pages of this book, spending time engaging with the unique and diverse animal life that occupies this island and its surrounding waters hopefully has enriched your life forever. It may seem grandiose, but the connections we share with the creatures on this island extend to all of the individuals living on this planet.

The relationships humans have with each other and with other species has a long and convoluted history. Regardless of your beliefs, religion, gender, nationality, or species, we are all made up of cells containing DNA. It's the DNA in our cells that dictates what our role on this planet will be, though it feels like we humans are something more, that we're special. We have choices. We are capable of empathy, understanding, faith, and forethought.

Sadly, humans are also susceptible to greed in ways that no other animal has matched. Preparing for the future and hoarding resources is nothing new in nature, but we have degraded, decimated, polluted, and eliminated habitats for people, animals, and plants alike on account of our unchecked greed. This has not been to our own benefit.

Nevertheless, we have also done more to enhance our existence than any other species on Earth. We can deal with issues, make informed decisions, change our behavior, and plan for future generations. Have we not brought endangered species back from the brink of extinction, stabilized the ozone hole, and cleared our skies of choking smog from factories? *Yes*, and we've accomplished other seemingly impossible feats as well. By studying and mimicking nature, people have learned to create drinking water from the ocean through desalination, harnessed the energy of the sun in solar panels, manufactured airplanes that fly hundreds of miles in the sky, built bridges that span thousands of feet across rivers, and fashioned the most exquisite art from hunks of metal like gold and silver.

The problems we face in the decades that follow are not unsolvable. Some of our most amazing inventions have come about by copying nature; we need to continue to look to the natural world for guidance, inspiration, and solace. The solutions we seek begin with understanding, empathy, and a desire to make a difference.

Now it's time we focus our attention on *this*: how do we live lightly yet securely on the planet while honoring the right of all species to have their place in it as well? But it's not just a moral or philosophical issue. We need to remember that every species creates strands in the web of life. By allowing the removal of more and more species, whether by complacency, greed or neglect, we erode the integrity of the entire web.

Let's heed some advice of Aldo Leopold, who wrote in his landmark book, *A Sand County Almanac*, "The first rule of intelligent tinkering is to save all the parts."

DAILY BIODIVERSITY TREASURE HUNT

(with a little St. John culture thrown in)

Day One: Cruz Bay and VIERS

_____ Bougainvillea on the side of the road

_____ A termite nest in a tree.

_____ A boat that has a cool name: _____

_____ A Brown Booby flying

_____ A Frigate Bird harassing another bird

_____ A pelican (perched or flying)

_____ An iguana on the beach in Cruz Bay

_____ A feral chicken walking around Cruz Bay

_____ A taxi with a beautiful paint job

_____ The melodious sound of a frog chirping

_____ A goat, sheep, and/or donkey

_____ A deer at the beach

_____ A mongoose scurrying

_____ A Fishing Bat

_____ A Soldier Crab

Day Two: Little Lameshur and Yawzi Point

_____ A sea turtle

_____ A Four-Eye Butterfly Fish

_____ A Long-Spined Sea Urchin

_____ A juvenile damselfish

_____ A Slippery Dick

_____ Mermaids Fans and/or Neptune's Shaving Brushes

_____ A Sergeant Major

_____ A French Angelfish

_____ Fire Coral

_____ An Organ Pipe and/or Turk's Cap Cactus

_____ Frangipani Tree (and you must smell the flower!)

_____ An Elkhorn Coral

_____ Blue Tangs in a school

_____ French Grunts in a school

_____ A Trunk Fish (smooth or spotted?)

_____ A Spotted Eagle Ray

Day Three: Greater Lameshur, Europa Bay, and the Dock

_____ Sea Grape trees, Acacia, and Coconut palms

_____ Any species of parrotfish

_____ A Bristle Worm

_____ A Christmas Tree Worm

_____ A Spaghetti Worm

_____ A Lionfish (remember—no touching!)

_____ A Yellow-tailed Snapper

_____ The Tektite Museum

_____ Land Crab or Fiddler Crab

_____ Genip trees

_____ Pinguin or Wild Pineapple

_____ At least five different shells of mollusks

_____ Bioluminescence

_____ Plankton

Day Four: Salt Pond Bay, Ram Head, and Drunk Bay

_____ Ground Doves

_____ The view from the top of Ram Head

_____ A Peacock Flounder

_____ A Southern Stingray or a Nurse Shark

_____ Black and Yellow Gobies

_____ A Red-Lipped Blenny

_____ The Salt Pond

_____ Hermit Crabs (a.k.a. Soldier Crabs)
_____ Coral sculptures (Did you make one, too?)

Day Five: Haulover Bay and Hurricane Hole
_____ Stoplight Parrotfish
_____ Princess Parrotfish
_____ Purple Sea Fan, and a Flamingo Tongue
_____ Brain Coral
_____ Doctor Fish, Surgeon Fish, and a Blue Tang
_____ A Baby Barracuda
_____ A Trunk Fish
_____ Bar Jacks
_____ A Spiny Lobster
_____ Red Mangroves and their prop roots
_____ An Upside-Down Jellyfish
_____ Staghorn Coral
_____ Star Coral
_____ Red, Blue, and Green Sponges, encrusting
_____ A Black Ball Sponge or a Vase Sponge

Day Six: The Petroglyphs, Reef Bay, and Booby Rock
_____ Bridled Quail Dove
_____ Scaly-Naped Pigeon
_____ Zenaida Dove
_____ Crested Anole
_____ Barred Anole
_____ Striped Anole
_____ Grass Anole
_____ The Petroglyphs
_____ The Sugar Ruins at Reef Bay
_____ The Antillean Fruit Bats (look up in the rafters)
_____ A Dusky Damselfish
_____ A Yellow-tailed Damselfish
_____ A Mutton Snapper
_____ A Margate or a Gray Snapper
_____ A Caesar Grunt

_____ A Nassau Grouper

_____ A Trumpet Fish

Day Seven: Leinster Bay and Waterlemon Cay

_____ A Maho Tree

_____ A Love Bug

_____ A sea cucumber (and maybe a brittle star)

_____ Pin Cushion Sea Star

_____ A big barracuda

_____ A school of Silversides

_____ A sea turtle (Green or Hawksbill)

_____ The view from Annaberg

_____ An octopus midden

_____ How many yachts were in Leinster Bay?

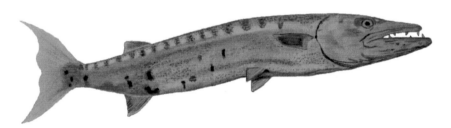

Great Barracuda

HELPFUL GUIDEBOOKS

For General Snorkeling (fish and other stuff)

Humann, Paul, and Ned DeLoach. 1996. *Snorkeling guide to Marine Life Florida Caribbean Bahamas.* Jacksonville, FL: New World Publications. ISBN: 1-878348-10-8.

Burkhold, Robert. 2007. *Reef Fish & Coral USVI.* Bob's Beach Photography. For more information, go to bobsretreat.com.

For Fish, Sea Creature, and Coral Guides

Humann, Paul, and Ned DeLoach. 2013. *Reef Fish Identification: Caribbean Bahamas South Florida.* Travel Edition. Jacksonville, FL: New World Publications. ISBN: 978-1-878348-45-6.

Humann, Paul, and Ned DeLoach. 1994. *Reef Creature Identification: Caribbean Bahamas South Florida.* New Jacksonville, FL: New World Publications. ISBN: 1-878348-01-9.

Humann, Paul, and Ned DeLoach. 1994. *Reef Coral Identification: Caribbean Bahamas South Florida.* New Jacksonville, FL: New World Publications. ISBN: 1-878348-456.

Kaplan, Eugene H. *Southeastern and Caribbean Seashores.* Peterson Field Guides. New York: Houghton Mifflin. ISBN: 0-395-97516-6.

Mangroves

Rogers, Caroline. 2011. *The mysterious, magical mangroves of St. John, U.S. Virgin Islands.* ISBN: 978-0-615-54751-0.

Birds

The various habitats on the island lend themselves to bird watching, and the National Park Service provides a great little pictorial guide that you can download from the Web at www.nps.gov/viis/learn/nature/upload/viisbirdchecklistphotoguide.pdf.

Websites

Terrestrial plants and animals of the Virgin Islands
http://www.smilinglizard.com

General St. John Information

Gaffin, Pam. 2013. *St. John Feet, Fins and Four Wheel Drive.* Amer Paradise Pub, July 2001. ISBN: 978-0963106094.

Singer, Gerald. 2013. *St. John Off the Beaten Track.* St. John USVI: Sombrero Publishing. ISBN: 978-0-9790269-2-8.